JOHN TRANTER is a leading contemporary English-language poet. He has published over twenty collections of verse and several anthologies and has given more than a hundred readings and talks around the world. He has visited New York City over twenty times, and has lived in London, Melbourne, Singapore, and elsewhere, and is now based in Sydney. He is the founding editor of the free internet magazine *Jacket* (*jacketmagazine.com*, now *jacket2.org* at UPenn), and the founder of the Australian Poetry Library project (*poetrylibrary.edu.au*) which publishes over 40,000 poems on the Internet. He is also the founder of the free *Journal of Poetics Research* at <http://poeticsresearch.com>, and he has a personal journal at <johntranter.net>.

HIS JOURNAL AND HIS HOMEPAGE at *johntranter.com* feature over a thousand pages of poems, articles, reviews, interviews and critical material, including reviews of this book and extensive notes to many of the poems in it.

Also by John Tranter

Monographs:

Parallax
Red Movie
The Blast Area
The Alphabet Murders
Crying in Early Infancy: 100 *Sonnets*
Dazed in the Ladies Lounge
Selected Poems (1982)
Under Berlin
The Floor of Heaven
At The Florida
Gasoline Kisses
Different Hands (fiction)
Late Night Radio
Blackout
Ultra
Heart Print
The Floor of Heaven
Borrowed Voices
Studio Moon
Trio
Urban Myths: 210 *poems: New and Selected*
Ten Sonnets

Anthologies and compilations:

The New Australian Poetry
The Tin Wash Dish (poetry)
The Penguin Book of Modern Australian Poetry (co-editor)
Martin Johnston: Selected Poems and Prose

Heart Starter

101 New Poems 2015

John Tranter

Puncher & Wattmann

Heart Starter, 2015

Published by Puncher and Wattmann, Sydney
Printed in Australia

Book design by John Tranter and David Musgrave
Cover art by Louise Hearman: Untitled 23723-1998-oil-on-masonite-69x91cm, by permission of Liz Laverty.
Back cover photograph of the author in Sydney, 2009, by Anders Hallegren.

First Australian Edition
ISBN: 9781922186560

Puncher & Wattmann
ABN 94 002 569 507

Net: http://www.puncherandwattmann.com
Email: puncherandwattmann@bigpond.com
Postal: P.O. Box 441, Glebe NSW 2037

This project has been assisted by the Australian Government through the Australia Council, its arts funding and advisory body.

Australian Government

Australia Council
for the Arts

Much that is beautiful must be discarded
So that we may resemble a taller
Impression of ourselves.

John Ashbery, *'Illustration'*

ACKNOWLEDGMENTS: Venues and sometimes dates of publication for each poem are listed in the *Notes to the Poems*, starting on page 139. Acknowledgment for prior publication is due to the editors of the following publications:

The Melbourne *Age*, the *Australian*, *Australian Book Review*, the *Battersea Review* (London), the *Harvard Review*, *La Traductiere* (Paris), *Mascara* magazine (online only), the *North-East Review* (Boston, USA), *Otoliths* magazine, *RABBIT* magazine, *Southerly* magazine, the *Steamer* (ed. Sam Langer), the *Sydney Morning Herald*, the *Times Literary Supplement*, *Van Gogh's Ear* (USA).

'747 Sonnet' was published as a broadside poem by Desmond Kon at Squircle Press in Singapore in July 2013. 'Crowded Hour' and 'The Consonants' were published in *The Best Australian Poetry* 2013 edited by Lisa Gorton. Ten sonnets ('The Love Song of J. Edgar Hoover', 'Tasman Sonnet', 'Poem beginning with a Line by John Anderson', 'Heroic Story', '747 Sonnet', 'Detour', 'Far North Farm', 'Crowded Hour', 'The Consonants', and 'Poem beginning with a Line by Basil Bunting') were published in the chapbook *Ten Sonnets* (Vagabond, Sydney) on 29 September 2013.

I owe special thinks to Lyn Tranter and to Andrew Riemer for their astute practical criticism, and to Brian Henry at the University of Richmond, Virginia, for his scholarly research into the contemporary use of the Terminal, in which form are written the poems in Sections One and Two.

Contents

SECTION TWO 73

SECTION THREE 99

Author's Preface

THIS, my twenty-fourth book of poems, is made up of three sections: some poems related to *The Best of the Best American Poetry 2013* (Series Editor, David Lehman, Guest Editor, Robert Pinsky), some poems related to *The Open Door: One Hundred Poems, One Hundred Years of 'Poetry' Magazine* (Don Share and Christian Wiman, Eds., 2012), and thirty or so poems, mainly rhymed sonnets, written by me in recent years. The poems in the first two sections appear in this book loosely in the order in which the 'originals' appear in those two collections of mainly North American verse, except where the usual order has been changed to allow for a poem running to more than one page to appear on facing pages. Ten of the sonnets in part three appeared in my chapbook *Ten Sonnets*, Vagabond, Sydney, 2013. For all the poems, any significant notes and derivations are listed in the Notes to the Poems, at the end of the text.

In the first two sections, I chose to write Terminals; that is, I started with drafts which borrowed the end-words of each line of some poems in each of the two books concerned. I then changed the position of the line breaks in a few of my new poems and in a few cases changed the original line-end words, partly to be spared the annoyance of poets who might resent my using 'their' line-endings as my own, and partly because I felt that my using some of the words ending each line would lead to pointless contortions; words which ended some lines in some poems didn't present much in the way of inspiration, and others were too strongly rhymed.

Section One

Algernon Limattsia

Thanks, I'm feeling a lot better.
Yes, it may have been the weather –
unseasonable this year with its excess of feathers
mingled with show and shit, rotten weather
to select for our anniversary get-together,
first time in a month of Sundays, pissy weather
that makes you feel like dressing all in leather
and doing a rain-dance, not that the weather
would notice that; a hat full of feathers
would be fine too, whatever the weather.
Then dress for the heat and head out to the double-header
game. Do you ever think of the weather
in Ireland, the chill fog, the half-drowned Irish Setter
gambolling over the soaked grass in the wet weather?
No? Thinking of the old data terminal, the feathers
that adorn it, and outside the Californian weather
shining on us all, creditors and debtors
alike, all smiling in the smiling weather
we feel nostalgic for, writing air mail letters
about it to Mom, myself a little under the weather,
entering incorrect data like a data dissenter
on the fringe of the Army. This weather
a fellow can't be blamed for dressing in feathers
to keep cool. Yeah, I hear he's a weather
man on the new TV station, embarrassed by mentors
in every direction. No, he just predicts the weather –
that is, he reads out what the meteorologists and other
                    inventors
make up on the day. They know nothing about the weather,
they just pretend to – now he's broadcasting from the center
of a twister – hurricane, sorry – this hot summer weather
sure gets me confused. Are they your feathers?
What shall we do in this indescribable weather?

My Sister

My sister feels sexy
today, she says. I think she just feels needy
as usual. Those guys on the porch, tell them
to piss off. Why? Because
if you feel needy, who needs you?

Needy is like greedy, let's not pretend
it's just a rhyme like 'got' and 'hot'. You
know rhymes exist for a reason, like lying
down after lunch in the heat or lying to them
about what you
said you did last night: you're not so hot,
Honey. South of the Border
you might be a pole dancer

or some señorita in need,
but not here, understand?

Go then to Mexico, be
honest, say what you really mean
to them,
those men on the porch, be sweet
and be
yourself, be a thing-in-itself

itself, and I'll be a thing-for-you
in case you need Some Thing
other than my regard, the thing you can't
really ask for, the thing you
hate about the heat, that you can't

turn off, South of the Border it's hot.

The Puma in the Duma

In my dream I was surrounded by seraphs
wearing morning suits, looking at me
quizzically in the crowded Parliament. Then I was being chased
by a Russian mountain lion who drooled a lot
then I was being covered in a forest of hands,
then just gloves, swarming all over me
like a furious blanket. Take care,
said the concierge, rattling her keys. No excuses,
now, no dallying with your desire
for a hot chocolate, no tales to the elected members about
how you were late because of the thousands of motes
that clouded your eyesight, though
your eyes were working fine yesterday, days ago,
weeks ago, why, I spotted you reading the papers
in a café just down the street, it was ordained
that someone see you, all by itself
it ordained itself. Don't listen, they're liars,
all of them, crowding the Assembly, each
one the worst of them, full of a passionate intensity.
Don't you feel that? Employ the First Gear first,
then the Second, and so forth, driving on
the gravelled path at first, then erratically onto the lawn,
ruining the flower-beds, squashing the loaves of bread
laid out for the inhabitants of the dream –

gosh, I'd forgotten that, the flush of madness
that made you dream of a dribbling puma, itself
slightly crazy, drooling just a little
at the memory of its several selves
and their good electoral intentions,
how its very best intentions always get
changed horribly into some kind of bad memory,
like the time it attacked a harmless gnome
that was guarding the garden. Who instructed
you to grab your whip and then frighten it
so that it ran off into the night, so that it
was caught frozen in the approaching headlights,
the darkness filled with nothing but its empty roar?

Robed With the Cloth of Gold

God I was bored!
Bored like a solid wooden log,
stuck for hours holding
those wooden boards
while you pounded and pounded
at the nails, rows
of identical nails (God I was bored).
Then the time we went back
to the boatshed full of old boats
and you tried to repair the broken wheel,
whacking at it
while I held it upright, looking
out the window at my small
cloud of boredom, gunwales
nailed into place, wooden seat
nailed into place, the sand granular
on the beach, covered with smelly sea-fans
and a few greying
corpses of fish, my neck
aching with boredom. Sometimes
I just sat for hours doing
nothing much, carrying
your bag of nails, watching paint drying
and trying not to be bored, like what
gave you the idea I'd jump at
the chance of exploring those old tunnels
that went nowhere? You pointed
at the ocean – look,
you said, it may seem boring, but under
the horizon there's a much sunnier
place, an island full of coconuts, often
clangorous with birdsong,
even the natives get
excited at the birdsong – but to
get there we need a boat, though

it doesn't seem to be coming on so well, or
maybe I should just give up – God I'm bored,
you admitted, I admit I'm much
more bored than you. I smiled: So now you know.

In Junction Junction

Just look, will you, at those old buildings...
Laid out side to side, it never seems to end:
Café, Hamburger Joint, Credit Union, High School,
Junior School, Hardware Store, General Store, and Bank.

Just what for the Love of God would possess
anyone to build that stuff, that library, that temple
to common sense. It might seem to make sense now,
when you can see the usefulness of the Railway Station by

the Parking Lot, and so forth, each
with its purpose, the Soda Fountain beside the Movie Palace
and so forth, but when there was nothing there but time
and endless sunlight, nothing growing, no grass, not

enough of anything, why, who could see their way through
to building things from the inside right to the outside,
one beside the other, who could believe it?

Intuition

Here I am in New York at last, full of distress
that it should be so fucking hard,
this city life I embraced so
enthusiastically at first, like
smiling constantly,
every day a picnic
from one end of the neighbourhood
to the other, oh yeah,
all the dirty dishes
magically cleaned, not this.

No, not this simple,
not like a funeral plot
under the waving yellow
willows, distant children's laughter
and my friends, all of them
gathered... no ifs and no buts.
Just mix me a Screwdriver,
hold the juice.
At the altar I tied the knot,
at the gallery I became the art
and everyone stared at my muumuu
and me in it, ice cubes
clinking, I'm not a simple
girl of female or woman,
like Mother, why be scared of her?

Will you join me at mass?
Okay, don't. Look at them,
the way they transmogrify
pretty girls into hags,
a sweet filly into a nag,
a mermaid into a sea-
hag (Popeye). Just keep your eye on
those young pretty ones
lying in the glare of the sun.

The Animals

Every seventeen years they emerge, seventeen
is a prime number, those dumb cicadas,
how do they do it? How, in that tiny head,
that insect brain, in the long underground night,
how can they possibly be expected to
work that out? Maybe it's because the prime numbers
save them – by hiding underground
for ages they breed, and avoid the police.

Okay, six tigers. Several brown bears,
and a couple of little worms.
That should keep them happy – oh,
and some quills to write home with.
Stop that! Get lost, will you? Okay, I have
a lack of eagles – let's see if we can get
some eagles, at least a few of them.
Okay, four old eagles
and a packet of bird seed,
I think I have some bird seed, yes,
no problem. Oh, look at that eagle pass
silently overhead!

The ghost in the haunted room pretends to be a librarian.
It haunts me, then the whole town, then you. It came in,
then it left. In the old library, lots of angels are asking for
book loans, they want to borrow books. Thanks to her.

Harry, that can of white paint, can you please see if
you can find it for me, and the other material
I need. Stop! That's enough! Now
I'll just have to carry it for miles and miles.

Now they'd like me to fill in the form:
birthplace, right here. Gender, as usual,
occupation, God knows.
For a date, write 1943.
You know what? Sometimes you look like me,
afraid that someone like you will paint
all the buildings in the town, and

down in the street – here she comes,
in her high heels, heading for her room –
You know what? Sometimes
it's hard to remember to open
that door to the distant past.

I've had this dump. I think I'll go to Paris.
Okay, go then. In the hotel, inside the front bar
is a total stranger who wondered at the rippling
effect of the light through the curtains.
He has American dollars, he likes these hotels,
and travelling around Europe, he thinks we are
a little parochial, yet the town is not without charm,
he ventures, looking like the handsome stranger
in the fortune-teller's tale, he wears Ivy League clothes
and tousled hair, he often goes right to sleep in
hotel bedrooms on those long journeys
through Europe's towns and along the canals.
This peripatetic life I've led, he says,
where has it got me? A dozen years to the day
I've been searching for her, boy, I'm ready to give up.
You could say I have accumulated holiday leave,
and sick leave, huh! It's strange, the more I dream of her
the more her image changes; one day an angel, then
some kind of horrid monster warns me off. It's less like
love than warfare. Tell me, is there a future for us?
Okay, tell me how, if you will, tell me why
and for God's sake tell me what it's all about, when
I don't know what knocks me to the ground, what
is going on, why that dazzling light?
This place is inhabited by a devil, he says. I wait by the
window, by the door, massive light floods in, it's the devil
come to call, he promises me no harm, he will say whatever
comes to mind, plausibly say whatever takes me in.

Then later, it's so quiet, you can hardly hear him.
Really, he doesn't make a sound. He hides out there,
where the woodpecker hides from the world,

where the cloud hides from the busy day,
but soon enough it comes back to bother you,
or to bother your dreams, which is where it taps
into your fears, or your hopes. It opens the window
and peeps in to see if you're up, to ask you the time.

How I fell on the deck, how
when I was mortally hit
by my own arrow, how my left ear was
cut by the bowstring.

The archer drops his bow and rows.
I hear my own blood thump in my heart.
My heart is a piece of dead wood.
I have come home. So say I.

Three Lemons

I have to hand it to him, it astonishes me
they way he turns it from a sequence of noises
into a handful of lemons.
Isn't it amazing? Boy, if I were him
I just wouldn't know how to do it.
Unlike me, he takes this heap of cheap ideas,
eating food, drinking drink, smoking, sex,
and in the blender of his art he turns it
into a handful of damned lemons!
Some musician! Look at him, there,
sitting and thinking on the can,
those musical notes, all he can get,
turning them all into a lemon!

Not me, with my rotten childhood I wasn't meant
to grow into a composer. My father,
damn him, he despised me most days,
he thought I was the stupidest kid
in the whole world, he never thought his way
of turning everything I said into dreck, of
turning my speech into cacophony, of acting
monster to a child and his being the most horrible
parent, would matter – his belief was, I was the worst
thing to issue from his penis.
So shit on him.

Now he's dead, thank God, I listen to that
composer, what's his name, I'm stuck
remembering his name, starts with
P, B, no... I have a real home now, I'm in
clover, and I don't miss parenthood
one bit. I'm glad I'm not a father, a dad,
d'you hear? Peace, and a little music, no more
racket and chaos, we're as happy as
two June bugs, aren't we, you and I?

Small Town

You are mad to mourn alone. – Anne Carson

In this town, death creeps day by day
and claims a victim each day.
This is the Small Town of the Blank Wall
where a monster came and went
and where another walked up and down the road.

This is the Small Town of the Useless Police,
who do nothing, protect us from nothing.
It's too hard, they complain, and empty spaces
grow between their solid words of complaint,
their grievous anguish.

Stand up straight. Learn how to be a real man.
This is the Small Town of the Empty Windows
that watch us from a distance. The old man
walks before the cruel child, who quickly grows into
his own father, and shoots from hiding.

But here is not here, it is nowhere. It is where
you know you must be very quiet:
outside the town a frightened rabbit
hops across the highway.
There is nothing on or in the old wood stove.

Killing people out of town is not a sin,
not if a properly elected government asked
or ordered you to do it. As for us, it's different for us.
As for you, weak you, you might as well go
to where the cold moon shines on the forests.

On the moonlit pampas, they take out their knives
and stare at me. A century or more I have waited
for this man with the knife, who listens carefully
to the wind, with his weapon, who takes aim
and impales the moonlight itself.

When I was twenty-five I had learned to say no
to the ugly man with his huge questions and his sack of
stuff, and his tales of blackness waiting just outside
town, outside the world. I wonder
if I really can say no,

no to the deep water running out, under the moon,
its blade of light flickering on the water,
a threat. Like this ugly man who brings
his dark questions and doesn't tell it
like it is.

They ordered me to stop, so I did – where
the river runs deep. Now, I say nothing, when
I have a secret to keep, two words,
like the words 'his car', that I saw
in back of the dark woods.

Sorry; my mistake. Wow, what a lovely day!
Your breakfast is ready: coffee, bacon and
two poached eggs. The cowboys stored
their dreams and hopes where
all the useless hopes were,

otherwise they might become lost in the current
where the little twig wobbles back and forth,
pointing at me, then at you. Yes, it's a lovely day.
I'll tell you what: you pause,
and I'll nip into town.

See the gopher run back into his hole?
The running motion proves he's alive.
Yes, like you, he has a mother
who thinks of him every single day.
To her, he's like a nest-egg of solid gold.

A Pompeiian Aristocrat Considers the Future

1

Staring in the mirror... it's exhausting
To stare, but why? Anyway, it's me
As cool and still as a piece of statuary
Though a little better dressed, being
Alive, more or less. What a pain
To have to dress every day, to have
Hours to fill, puzzles to fathom,
Crowds of totally unknown people to disdain
Day by day. I'm not a silly girl
Who would make something of little me
And make a fuss of what I can see
Framed in a glass. There! A glass hurled
Out, a clever reputation quite severed
From my poor suffering self, forever.

2

It's not nearly enough. I don't care.
Sometimes in the dead of night, in my bitterest
Moments, tornadoes of self-censorship
Excepted, my whole life a colourful theater,
I resent the teachers strolling along the cool colonnades
And the trompe-l'oeil frescoes, the illusionistic
Illusions... well, I have to admit
I don't mind the way blues and reds
Shift into evening in the purlieus of my grotto
Here in the Tuscan countryside. Formalists
Take note: my grotto is a composite
Of Pope's at Twickenham, and some other ghetto
I remember from Venice, where I once lived
For a whole month quite undisguised.

3

Where was I? After breakfast, make
Do with who you are, Augustan
Quibbles aside. I'll have to accustom
Myself to a life as solitary and as chaste
As a statue's, on a plinth all by itself
Day after day, sunlight circulating, the last
Rays of the setting sun lighting on my clasped
Hands... watching a little black and white dog
Playing with a leaf, sere and red
From Autumn's onset. But a statue lacks a soul,
And cannot be consoled or unconsoled.
For a whole day, I'll live on the edge,
I'll live a life full, complete and whole,
Retiring at nightfall into my cave.

4

An angry style: furious with a whole life
Wasted, now the bother of being reborn
As a better person among the Roman ruins.
Glaring at my newborn urges, floodlights
Everywhere, what should I do?
Young men perform disgusting acts
With an innocence learned from Plato
But that was in another time, where happiness
Was brewed in a big pot on the campfire
Like coffee, and flickering shadows and real
Phantasms mingled in the Grecian sunlight.
A single file of women, with their horrid glances.
Time to pop back into my own skin
And be an innocent child, again, again.

Family

I'm just lyin' out back here, looking up at a cloud
floating in from the Pacific, over the crowd of sisters
and brothers baying for blood

at the cricket. One player lands a right hook
on the bowler's jaw, a punch of astounding force.
Now he's gone from the field.

Determination bears little relation
to righteousness, misery loves company
and desperation lives alone.

Lookit those children wriggling their toes
in the waterGosh, , and the mess
they leave us.

I heave them up onto my shoulders.
I pledge to hold to the center,
I promise we'll all turn left together

at the same time, on Monday morning,
we'll all drift back to earth.
Please be yourself down there;

you know how to go back home.
Who knows the most, knows the good soul
can hold the lost child,

can hold the vagaries within the family circle,
swing the children round and round, can
loose the bond and swing them back.

So tell them
I'll soon be gone,
that's all.

Let them dream their own quiet, still
dream of faith.
Time for me to go away.

Time for me to go home.
I have always been true
to you,

my readers, under the trees.
Down below, younger readers bring
hope, the one, two, three

of pleasure down there. They know me
to be human in my own way.
No burden, I hope, trying to be true

to you, plural, the way you do
leave a clue and then go
somewhere else, do I know

that place? It'll happen soon,
the empty room, the empty stair
to everywhere – then I'll know

it's time to go, time to forget
what meagre share
I ever had of the word,

but no matter what I missed
I had my reward:
this.

God Goes to Work

Oh, my keys are in the door,
aren't they? Every morning
more or less like this. Now where's my umbrella?
Wallet... uh, no money.
Gee, it's great to leave the house
at long last, head off to the city, heart
stuttering in admiration
at my good self. For example,
if I dream of an encumbrance,
a child, say, outside my hut
covered with coconuts, spoon
in mouth, fouled diapers...
no, let's dream of a better world.
I adjust my top-coat,
tighten my fashionable collar
around my nose –
neck, sorry – slight difficulty breathing
as I go uphill. My new saloon's tail-
lights gleam in the dusk – aside
from the way they gleam in the early morning
light. Tonight, remember to collect some food
from the supermarket, remember to be
on time, every time, your cool detachment
displayed for general admiration, your eager
nostrils flaring with excitement, your ears
flapping as everyone in the office welcomes
your arrival, at last, an unexceptionable god.

A Nipping and an Eager Air

Thou art alone, Horatio, alone.
Do not waver, do not stand there open-mouthed
gazing as the ghost upends the dish,
to drink, tips it up, drops it face-down in the dirt.
It's only china, only fine china, your chemise only laundry,
your laughter quite dry, the dying kingdom
unbearable. The Prince your Friend is quite
unhinged by it all, though gentle in his manners, gentle
in his speech to the ghost, though he'll retch
in the end, and die wretched.

Give him the meat of some poems, give him a song daily
to protect him from this epic poor treatment.
It is up to you after all, it shall be sprayed wet
by the waves at the foot of the battlements, it
shall take forever to resolve, it shall never
rest in a pine box as my fate, mine
alone, names its time and place. It
shall fledge itself and fly, fledge
its tiny, afraid soul – no – like a kitten, licked
by its mother religion and its father faith
crawl unfledged to bed to sleep.
The weight of the Kingdom, it
shall struggle and propagate,
give birth to horror, it shall sing of what it
fears most, the grave, deep down in the deep, it
finds a grave someone has dug
and there rests its heart half-heartedly,
and neglects to test the point of its sword,
neglects to polish the crest
on the crown, it calls its worst enemy a bastard
but has come to find a bastard death at the point
of a sword, it awaits your coming, you
come at last,
too late, you carry it,
your noble friend's body,
no more.

Regeneration

Between the chorus and the bridge I agree,
we are losers, between
the rhyme and the verse we followed
we became less and less available;
our code, lumber in sawmills,
our refrain, clutter in hospitals;
in drugs we trust
wiping the floor of some useful doctor's office
and spying through grimy windows
the joy coupling brings us
in the long, empty evenings
when the pursuit of happiness
is all we pursue.

Just look at us, dozing in the Great Halls
and eating in grubby restaurants
or maybe waiting on tables, hoping for some little extra
tip here and there. Such things define us,
such trinkets come to brand us.
Fluffy towels we admire, the crowded variety of the parked cars
returned to their owners who park behind the legend-makers
and hope they, too – hoping to gain access to the officials
who matter, in fact, not just in the hazy side-street
but in City Hall, clothed in fanciful imitation of the Mob,
threats unheeded by our generation, especially by us,

so why don't you come
join us followers?

Bare Skin

Isn't it lovely, lying on the grass
with this barefoot picnic atmosphere
in all directions? And so the pretty young girl
rushes off to the drugstore, and then returns

with an armful of drugs and soda cans. How do
you do, guys, she says, little tobacco shreds
on her lower lip, then she neglects
completely to put her gingham blouse on

at all, and in the strict sunlight her body
glows like a newly-discovered atomic element.
Sheesh! cry the guys, in unison, two of them all
together. The sunlight, slow and sticky, like balm.

What a cute pair of tits! The weather, it
is changing; chlorophyll trickles through the cells
of the grasses in the lawn, each green leaf
made up of millions of little molecules.

The breeze blew, just a little, the leaves breathed
in and out, the warm sunlight spilled
over the girl and the grass. Now she is old. Perhaps
she thinks of this perfect day, and remembers.

The Parkas

Let's say the old man lies in bed, very sick.
He listens to the radio, he reads
trash, his sleepy head nods
and the eyelids droop over his eyes.

He takes ages to unscrew
the failed bulb. Match heads
flare and go out. Of all his enemies, none
knows anything like this dull hunger,

which waxes and wanes, but is constant
generally. He looks out the window, but his sight
flickers and fails, and a slow faint groan
comes from him as he recognises the men in parkas

standing around below, staring
up at the blank window and down at the ground.
He's old, he must be eighty-five or ninety
and his frame looks diminished

by the weight of his crimes and of the world.
His muscles are flabby, his feeble cock
is of no use now, and his long loneliness
gives him nothing worthwhile. In the light

over the mirror he looks ashamed
of the bad things he's done, his criminal
past, his long, endless record
of violence. His thin smile excludes

all his true friends, all of that company,
his many lieutenants, his few trusted
pals, his forgiveness excludes each
one of them from his crowd of evil thoughts.

Is that what they call kindness, those ones
spared? He eats a cold slice of pie,
then he cleans the plate and puts it away.
He peels an orange, watching the curve

of the peel drop from the knife with a thunk
into the garbage bin. He tries to sleep,
not because he needs to, but because the world
won't leave him alone, otherwise.

The watching men simply disappear,
he stares for hours at his cock,
he carefully counts up his various hungers
and shuffles around in a small circle

on the rug. Soon he'll be just a body,
not a person. Soon he'll have his rest,
that he deserves. He's part of the Great Chain
of Being, God at the top, himself a mere X

down at the bottom. He looks at his hand,
it shakes a little. Some days he feels better,
so much so that he wants to celebrate
being alive, celebrate greed, praise gluttonous

appetites... Sure, he's a little self-forgiving,
who isn't? The weakness of the flesh
should be forgiven, otherwise the story
of his life would be endless self-recrimination,

what's the use in that? There's a noise, some
people in the hall, he should get out
of this death-trap, but he's a single
man, he has no 'loved ones' to go back

to, pleading, hands outstretched,
forgiveness for what? For leaving, for returning,
for the endless dark that follows the slamming
of the door, the door is open, slamming the door shut.

Doting on Blubber

Aren't they beautiful, those jellyfish?
Blubbing around in the pallid shallows,
like sallow reflections of the clouds.

I know you're thinking 'Is this guy all right?
Jellyfish? Uh?' But all God's creatures
deserve a rhyme or two. Like gluey sacks

of wet rubber, they seem
to be constantly shifting
shape. Like a Boy Scout troop

they seem to turn into their own cousins,
then quickly get down to business,
just blobbing around, their attention span

pretty brief, I guess, unlike
the endless thoughts that bother a blue balloon
as it floats through the sky and ends

up in some provincial park, an expanse
of dry grass and rubbish. My heart
goes out to these little fellers; each like a cauliflower

or an oversized, sperm-filled condom –
uh, maybe not – each like itself
sheltering in the watery shade,

looking a bit like a gluey parasol.
Funny, they're never featured as an opera's
main feature. Maybe they should disguise

themselves as a tangle
of flabby princesses? Recognition
eludes them, even as they turn into a trope

trapped in plastic bags of tripe, or something,
multiple identical brainless figures
of speech, a speech refiguring

how we all have a modicum of ectoplasm
inside us, that woolly stuff
ghosts exhale, you know, what ghosts do

in the dark. I don't really know
much about jellyfish, but don't
think I can't discourse on their metaphorical shape

riding like pirates on the ocean's swells,
slopping through the ugly algae blooms,
that's usually how they're described

by the average writer, an unlikely
luminous blancmange, like the chiffon
scarf that choked poor Isadora –

no, forget it. No individual style,
right? All sharing an appearance that binds
one to the next to another,

always together, never apart,
none ever able to look lovelier
than another, each blob shapeshifting

into the same old blob again, as –
looking for a fresher simile – words
fail me again, and a grave lack of grace

infects this whole unfettered
space, this unrealised form
where cheap words flower

like a drunk with Korsakoff's Syndrome at the theatre
or a giant with Tourette's Syndrome at the ballet,
ugly things spouting from his huge mouth,

but no, the page is full as the Bay is full
of smellyfish – sorry, jellyfish, a whole world
quivering into a jelly bowl shape.

All Souls College

I'd like a hundred pets, all of them named
something like Milly the Marmoset or
Cocky Rocky the Cockatiel or Flabberguts the Platypus.
And they'd never go to bed, but sit up and talk all night, signifying
nothing much except *et cetera*

blah blah how things have changed,
and run around with nothing on, disappearing in a sudden blink!
Take a French phrase like *de rigueur*,
it just means you yearn to sound sophisticated,
and you probably call your white cat 'Esquimaux',
and mourn the loss of the *Andrea Doria*, and the first

thing you think of this instant is how to get back into All Souls'
College when they have locked the gates
and you can't climb over the hedge,
too tall and prickly, and you're not sparkling so much now,
your star is fading into that awkward conversational silence
your tutor bestows on your ignorance.

Thanks heaps. My glowing promise plunges into an oubliette.
Oh well, I guess it's time to get down to the serious business
of being a College Tour Guide, showing hicks the sights.
One of which will not be the various pet creatures
I used to dream of while I was straining
to learn the words of the Old College Song.

I am the most promising child in this whole land.

A Man and a Woman

Okay, so you're a woman.
A beautiful woman, but not in
love with the idea of pulchritude
the way a 1950s woman
might want to be Marilyn Monroe, whereas
no, you know your limitations
and simply long to be – in spite
of the advertising industry – a woman,
no more or less, just you
yourself. Mind if I tag along?
Maybe we could go shopping
on Fifth Avenue, or take in a museum,

the one with de Kooning's 'Woman

I', 1953, or another painter, maybe someone
like the guy called Philip Guston, in fact
not his real name – maybe Mr Goldstein wanted
to be some other person, standing in
for some man standing in a shadowy doorway
of history: say Dien Bien Phu, 1954, when
Frank O'Hara was having breakfast
in the sunny kitchen at a friend's house
on Long Island in the summer, or maybe you
have not yet had yours,
so have it, now, please – and could I please come

too, and help you devour it?

How it Starts

You're walking along the boardwalk
beside your girlfriend,
and she's saying
'Will you check out
that lifeguard? Bad language
from top to bottom,
going up or going down,
let's get a little closer,
to the scene,' she says, 'before it
disappears taking him
with it, I think
he's just a part-time
lifeguard, he carries mail
in his weekday job, out
and about like Diana Ross
in love
with her new hit and its currents
in and out of the money system,
toting his mailbag and laughing
at the thought of being a lifeguard,
he can hardly swim.' 'Let's leave
this whole unpleasant situation,'
I say, 'before we have a fight
about it,' says
I, 'before you start nagging
and whining and nitpicking,
I mean, really,
he's just doing his job,' I say.
'Oh really?' says
my girl friend. 'then what do you say
about this guy, yes, him,
doing everything he can
to impress some dame?' I say –
reasonably – 'she's just some waitress

he picked up, not the first time
she's chatted to a lifeguard. Look, she's napping
on his lap – ooh –
boy!' I let out a low whistle
at the thought of him
sullying this girls's innocence.
Then he refills
his pipe, takes a bite of an apple pie,
so he looks like a regular saint.
'Look,' I say, 'Now will you admit
you're a shit?' 'What? me admit
I'm a shit? Shove it up
your...' Just then the lifeguard gives a limp
and reveals a crooked shoulder,
so I break down and cry enough for all of us.

Never Safe

You won't make old bones.
That signature, is that in your hand?
That writing, is that you again?
I know, it's something you have made,
once, long ago, then you did it again.
You want me to smile,
of all things, along the tracks
we make, the twigs broken
and the grass trampled, and over there
a bleached white skull
in the sun. Your eyes are open, then closed.
I can see your clothes have been washed
and dried, taken away and returned
to you here, clean. You frown, or
you give one of those harmless
looks, as though you really had
nothing to complain about, nothing
to be afraid of, again.

Now you eat from the common spoon,
the old dented spoon. Yes, an abundance
of good food, and yet I fear, and yet
somehow I think we're going to starve.
It's true that no one loves
a woman like she loves herself.
Have you had your St John's Wort
tablets yet? Where are your children?
You see, I am omitting
whole decades, a historical slippage
that easily separates
you the child from the who you are now. You'll figure
what I'm up to one day, anyway
you're still just a child
and this vale of troubles is your schoolyard.
Have you made a roll-call of your friends, a
roll-call of your enemies, a list
to memorise, Little Miss Hatred-on-a-Staircase?

Now you hide in your ornate designs
and your samplers and your tacky jewelry,
every plan a superfluity.
I remember when you were a child,
you and I and all of us lived
in a warm envelope of hope
that lasted through the long night hours
until the dark horizon was stained with light
and you rose up out of your childish fever
to pour out a bowl of water and wash
and we were all then in good health
and a cloud of mist traced our breath.
Now you tell a story with your wrong stitch,
how the little ones were ailing and mortal
and their lives just petered out.

It seems you have never been my friend.
For the things you allowed to happen, you apologised
but that was not enough. Maybe you thought
if you just ignored the mess
and walked off to chat on the phone
it would be okay. Which
is really just such
a horrible thing to do, a failed alibi
if ever I saw one, or
your ugly face behind your pretty face...
then, it seemed years later,
after ignoring all the trouble I'd had,
ignoring the sour fatal smell of gas
in the kitchen, ignoring our Mother, her
anger, her fear, how she held fast
to all those bad decisions, altogether
lost, wrecked in the middle of her life, not safe
from any of those disasters... her likes,
counted up: a stable home,
a sound house, four-square
on its foundations, no debtors
to bother with – how closely
the neighbours watch us – the way credit's

just dissolving... but over here
in the future, her fierce regard
has gone into her grave, and her memory's just
something like a reflection, now. We made
the troubled journey to our new house.
Yes, our efforts have been useless,
but that doesn't matter: now I read,
in my dream, that we have both been wakened.

Congress, the State of Mind

So I went out and walked in the sun
and stared up at the bright blue sky and all
the birds flying around, all
those goddam birds, some called
'Binky' and some called 'Diecast'
and some just called 'Doodle-Bug',
and it came to me that this
place and its people was the very best, the
most perfect society, under one law,
you just had to sign your name on the form
and put your selfish personal wishes on hold
for a while, and make that pledge
to behave better and all that stuff
and right then, quick
as a flash, you got political power
and all the voting husbands and wives
with their thousands of democratic kids
in their millions of rented rooms,
why, they had it made.

Fernando's Hideaway

Quit babbling in Portuguese, just let me think
for a minute, will you? This thing
I have about Poets in Portugal,
not the corny old Poets of the World
Unite, just the Poets in Portugal...
Fernando, d'you think they mind
being restricted to a peninsula?
Didn't the British, for instance,
fight the Peninsular War? Like, the Empire State
is not a state at all per se, but a skyscraper
type of building per se, emblem of the new century
blah blah or maybe emblem of 1936 –
Was it built then? Let me think... Uh, no,
that was the Kavanagh Building in Buenos Aires, object

of architectural adoration. Okay, Pessoa,
great poet, I think you're better than at least 3
other poets added together, not their fault,
but you come from a foreign country
and are thus an alien – don't freak out
when I say 'alien', it's just a term, an aberration
perhaps – it's not the Portuguese manner
to use words like 'alien', okay, you have vistas
to write odes to, Senhor Multiple Pessoa,
so you hardly need to know the difference
between the Greek philosopher Socrates
or the English playwright Shakespeare –
no, 'William', maybe 'Guillaume', definitely not 'Walt',
that was some one else. Did I hear that you trifle
with history, communists and antiStalinists
and the Spanish Civil War and anticommunism
which is not often civil, rather somewhat
aggressive? Your various reputations?
Well, I hear they're doing pretty well
these days. Readers find it interesting
that you suddenly became several sextuplets
instantly and simultaneously

all with different names, a *sexophrenic*
mélange, you might say, hardly a popular
mode – I should know – of entering a trance state.
Or maybe your suitcase of personas was
an instance of runaway multiple personality, Pessoa
old chap – d'you mind if I address you in the English
manner? Old pal, old mate, old China
plate, in Cockney rhyming slang – Walt Whitman,
that's who I meant – of average height
though, like me, his immense immodesty
told him he was a Great Poet, like you, Pessoa.
I greet you at the midpoint, Senhor Pessoa,
of several careers and lots of languages,
which makes me feel, you know, a little anxiety,
as I have English and Yiddish got from a book
and a Noo Yawk accent which is reasonable
though not great. Finally, let's talk about 'influence',
for example I believe I amplify the ample tradition of Whitman,
though some might say shut up you're longwinded,
so'bye, your pal, Old Allen Skinsberg Schmessoa.

Pesca Land

Thanks: gin martini, straight up, no ice,
Shaken, just a little, not violently, not stirred,
Colorless, not purple and orange tie-dyed
If you don't mind. D'you have the time?
What? Is it? Jesus! Time for some action
Around here: a tar-pit of prose was
Bogging me down for a while. See?
Headaches everywhere, neck, jaw, forehead.
Just write it out, she said, make it reachable
By the Average Jerk. Another drink. Time,
Gentlemen, please. Is he closing the joint, in
Ten minutes? This guy walks in and
Looks around, just the usual crowd, but he was afraid,
Strangely afraid. Outside, wind and snow,
Maybe he should wait for it to blow over
Before he makes his long-awaited move.
The wind stops, then the forest fills with silence.
Then this guy, this lawman, this mysterious... this
Mister Whatever... Wait: his drink has evaporated
Under the hot lights. Outside just a few trees
Covered with a glacial layer of ice,
And in the silence, a clock ticks, time
Passes, an angel passes, just passing time
He said, a snapshot taken
And folded away swiftly: moving
Pictures, how much time is left
For him now? Slowly the days
Pass, sunlight sweeping across the room so it seemed
Time was light and movement. They were
There a minute ago, those guys... Can this be real?
He stared into the bottom of his glass.
A tiny label in reverse lettering spelled out 'Made
In China'. Faint tinkling sounds
Danced across the clearing: listen!

It may be late Fall, it
May be even Winter.
The snow-filled days are horribly
dark and long now, though
They bring with them a whole new world.
Blink, and it has passed
And you have missed it again, dang! Then
You notice that those old gingham curtains are faded.
A sign! And it seems the whole world
Has faded, faded away,
everywhere.

The Manifest

*'He was spoilt from childhood by the future, which he
mastered rather early and apparently without great
difficulty.'*
         – From Safe Passage, *a memoir by Boris Pasternak,
         quoted by John Ashbery.*

I guess this is the narrow
road to the deep north, this rutted
track through the woods
that winds and climbs up –
hey, will you let
me finish? Up through
brambles, over rocks, rattle of
the vehicle climbing up

and up... each photo a slice
of the light, of the time,
of the smiles of the passengers.
As it grows dark we have access
to the quite unearthly
glow of the radioactive soil
and the radioactive dust

that imprints everything, but
not the feathery
luminous prints... the
photographs that cannot be
properly touched
because of their radioactive entrances,
their half-spoken meanings replete
with the cries of
change, it's the 1960s, please, change.

And I might say 'and'
and I might say it again,
and then I might write 'and
then he sprang onto
the ground, and it was firm,'

#

and I might act imperial
and I might be cleverly invisible
and I might throw you a curve
ball and gaze for hours at the dust
that seems to gather on
everything, even the
reading lamp, and gaze at the back

of the paperback itself –
swimming into view like the
book title 'In Praise of Cowardice'
which is probably fictive,
or the prolonged
automotive carnage
of Rome – where am I? – of the gleam
along the edge of the silver platter
I was born with, as you look down
and down and down
and see the floor open,

open up wide
and a glare spills up, a glare of light
lighting the way for the god
to ascend, to appear in the real world, still
outside of art this seldom happens. Is it

the waiter? Will you pay the bill?

What? It doesn't add up?

Crowding in under the porticoes,
neighbours, poor people, children of
work and slaves of heaven –

they're everywhere, wearing the
face that looks just like a stone

or maybe it is really a stone
and please let's not hear the cry
that bleeds from the stone, the air
that surrounds the grimacing face,
the face made up of painful features

that shriek and cry and slide and slip
from the fear of hell to the
hope of paradise to the click
that says you're photographed, the

click that takes us through
the door that opens then shuts
then opens on a face called 'Veronica'
or 'Thomaso', hell and heaven. O let us guard
ourselves from the face that speaks
like bubbles forcing upwards through brine
with the words of Thomas Aquinas,
cruel words, so that it seems
we are two not four

and we shall have to meet at noon
at that fucking awful restaurant
where no one meets you and me, where I
meet at long last you,

where you
meet the other maiden
who apparently has been lost forever,
Jesus, you too?
Or is it too much bright light
from Nambibia to Rebibbia,
where the hairy people of the left
lift their
legs and arms
suppurating in the steamy
noonlight,
not to mention the moonlight, where
once again
the thousands
of faces
of the poor just

grew, like you
grew with the horrible fleshgrowth
of your face...

#

god, fresh air
is what I need, lifting myself up
from being so down,
becoming small
where I was powerful and large, there
where you
laughed and then screamed
as the shit hit the fan, so you do

what you must do... your muscle
clenched, the drug made a fake façade
where you and I really screamed,
stoned, hand in hand,
stoned, arm in arm,
where I thought I was really me
and you were really you... no, they...

uh, she became her
own self, through
following a path to the opening
between what she thought and what she knew
of dreams and of life,
a path that wound up and up
so that I had to carry
you, who knew not the sun,

who knew nothing of the infinite
behind the sun, the unbearable amount
of love and lust and sweaty skin.
Do I hear you say you don't have time
to track truth to the end of the arcade?
Then why don't you just piss off

and render unto Caesar
all the small change
left by the merchant

of death-dealing small arms,
the merchant whose view is perfectly clear,
who sees like Father what matters and what
doesn't matter at all. Follow that star,

faint signal for a wise man.
Excuse me while I make a little note.
Well, here comes the sun, lifting

over the horizon, bearer of unbearable light
into and over the world, it
pours an unconscionable amount
of pure light, much more
than I deserve. Fly home, inhale, then
in the literary world it's dog eat dog.
It's time for a competition, the longest
competition in the world, one blink
and you're dead, that's what it says.
Write your poem on parchment, make a cross, spit
over your shoulder, lift yourself aloft

into the pure uncontaminated air
where the judges inscribe a single note
of approbation on the wind,
and wait and wait until it's your turn in
the Palace of Art, walls draped with brocade,
where acrobats dance in midair

and a chorus of whispers tells it
like it is at last: I always win! I mend

that rent in the garment of art again
and again, and, writing, I put a face

on the face of love.
Let me speak of that
which again and again
causes the door to open
and the reluctant student, lazy pupil
to sail away...
Here I have invented
the Art of Love, invented

among the colours and the dreams all swirling
forever a contaminated and powerful line
that promises me I'll be what I want to be.

Borodino

I don't mean to pry, John, but I was just checking
whether you have read that letter of Lermontov's –
to committ a double genitive – in the Petorin
translation, undergoing the usual transition
from Verily to Veracity to Vera
and several disinterested others.
No? I guess I left out of the reckoning
the fact that you may have preferred Tolstoy
and his tedious moralism, and one day change
your mind completely, and John – then
I discover a volume of Byron on your kitchen table –
Aagh! The scullery? Quite the wrong room!
Remember our holiday in Tuscany? How you held
onto me, clutching, until I threw you off!
Did you feel the sting in the scorpion's tail?
Did you let your idle hand
wander among the drawer full of knives
until it found the scorpion,
until flush with horror you yelped?

Poor young Lermontov: shot dead, he fell
and lay on the grass lightly
as though he was old, and just trying
to sleep a little, to rest, the door
to death creaking on its hinge, feeling tired,
exhausted from all that writing, all that happiness.
John, did you hear me, John?
What did I say? Oh, nothing.

American Prophecy

The car ports made of aluminum
and automobiles in the tin garages
shine and glitter, the sun may explode
into hot green summer,
crowds of teenagers fill the malls
and the packed roadhouses
where whole families eat crab cakes
and throngs of campers pump up and light
their kerosene lamps
in the soft American twilight...

But you in your comfortable cottage reject
the entire economic argument
capitalism is based on. The room grows bigger,
the water-glasses are crystal by Waterford,
short stories courtesy of Uncle Remus,
they all enlarge into a huge 'no contest'
case against Communism, which was made
in tired old Europe. You easily reject
the campfires and the lamps and the matchboxes
leaving only the darkness covering them.

Now whole families are vomiting
together, they gobble Valium
tablets, Table Talk Chicken Thighs
pile up on the bedside table in pyramids.
A thousand recruits are saluting
the President, their fate writ on the cloth-of-gold
that flutters above the town square.
A waving prairie of corn ripens,
and sorghum and miles of golden wheat
waving all the way to Oregon.

The old people know that they have to die,
the young people know it in their chairlifts,
in a rock crevice the stink of rib-bones
and old skin, a rusting car skids across
the centre line of the two-lane blacktop

and ends up in the ditch afire,
a surgeon throws his instruments in the autoclave
and forgets to disinfect them, columns of hot air
rise into thermals above the hexagonals
of gardens in the plaza and the attendant snails.

A pretty woman with armfuls of chrysanthemums
bumps into a dazed Ronald McDonald
on a sunny Sunday morning, he's wearing
a clown suit; fire pours from the aqueducts;
hideous wooden creatures are built by carpenters.
In the jungle a triumphant leech engorges
itself on human blood, students surrender
and are corralled into a deserted atrium
where they are harangued by a chef named Marc
until they swear to become more reliable.

Crowds of young people throng the malls,
young men and women dazed by a peculiar idleness
enforced by random choice and a lottery's lot,
drawn up in the back rooms of old motels
by executives familiar with petrochemicals
and the general stink of the neighborhoods of Tucson;
headmasters thrash the idle girls and boys
under their charge until their spinning brains
jerk out of control and run down
like broken clocks in dusty backyards.

These are the machinations and this is the machinery
of night, the soil ripped up by ploughs
and their upright sharpened steel colters,
as families and their children run for shelter,
living for a little in hiding, and then dying
in plain view, some of them wandering
still through the avenues and creekbeds of desolation,
their souls and brains fitfully illuminated
by visions of abnegation and naked bodies
and the motors spinning and the gears idle.

Here a happy fisherman hauls in a pickerel
and the field of water he floats on flames and burns,
the riverside grass is full of running rats,
an old man on a stool at a grindstone sharpens
his rusty scythe and hacks into the poppies
that splash their crimson everywhere, policemen
fully armed and in ranked blue lines march out
but those they wish to arrest are hiding in bombshelters;
a hundred-tonne mine under the distant ridge explodes
and ten thousand are killed, leeches engorge

their shiny bloat, a young man starts to dress
as the historical President Abraham Lincoln
and the audience breaks into sobs
as the Gettysburg Address sprays over them,
young husbands and younger wives all together
and their clutches of friends and their many children;
some calm and dazed, some frightened out of their skin
as they all go down with magistrates and judges
and lawyers and idle traffic policemen and acrobats
down into the crackle of flame, burning maple and birches

roaring with heat. This is the final dumbshow
where at last the striving young executive
gets his chance, but no chance; sobbing into their pillows
young wives in every similar suburb
from Springfield Illinois to Springfield Maine
ask what was it all about; their male children turn
from sulky failures into boys with possibilities, athletes
with half a chance at the big time; kids throw rocks
at big shiny cars on the freeway, millennia
pass and flame consumes the arrogant cities.

Righteousness fills to the lip a vase of pale alabaster;
promising children with the gift of the gab give up
and spend what's left of their lives in idleness,
gathering in small knots on the edge of deserts
and populating the dry islands,

their conversation repetitive and gassy.
The young wife tries on the peppermint striped skirt
and cleans her kitchen and her husband admires it;
she cooks an apple pie filled with baked apples,
life, death, innocence, and the blood of the lamb.

Boston Café

On your plate sausages and mash,
on the spoon a film of grease,
in your gut a meal to digest,
the floor covered with sawdust.
Turn the corner, you'll find an education
where the Harvard undergrads dazzle
with wit, e.g. in New York how Frank leaned
against the john door and the music went
dah de dah in the Five Spot, the man
playing the piano, Mal Waldron, may
earlier, have visited the toilets,
now he plays for Lady Day. Go on, stare
until your eyeballs become stiff.
On the kitchen sink, snail trails.
Do you have the stomach
to eat that stuff on the plate? Swallow it down
and the coffee too. A drunk comes in,
weaving his way from the sidewalk
to his stool, see the early sun shine
through the glass, the wobbling motion
and the flair with which
the guy pours the coffee, the mound
of food on the plate, now gone into your mouth,
then the chewing motion, then the swallow
as it goes down. Your body too
is just as full of juices,
is just as
keen to finish your last
cigarette before breakfast, to taste
that breakfast. Under the fluorescence
of the democratic lights you sat
that morning long ago, cooks
and crooks and cleaners and cabbies all
eating and drinking and chattering away,
getting ready for the coming day digestively
and, in their American way, getting it all down.

Picking on the Oil Company

Yes, I was going to piss on some petroleum
company for what they're doing to the environment,
Jesus, my children's environment,
and their greasy commercials
about the profound importance
of their deep ecological concern
and how they tread oh so softly
on the grass, those horrid oligarchs –
but it all feels so ineffectual,
like some self-indulgent self-semaphore,
one thoroughly committed person
signalling to another ready-to-be-committed person,
and it hardly seems to make any sense –
I mean, who cares what I feel
about something like a poor little lost kitty?
I think I'll just stay in bed
and count the discarded foreskins
of those horrible old men who drill and drill
looking for oil, for a fortune, honest,
then schlepp in to the bank.
Phew, I'm beat.
Another goddam year –
shopping list: don't forget eggs and flour
and milk – what a life!
But hey, don't get off your bike!
Hold your horses!
Corral the cows
back into the barn
that nestles at the foot of the hill,
join the local Methodist
Church, send your art to an art gallery
and get drunk in the nearest bar
and make love to your significant other
before I begin to swear
and things lose their value –
hey, before I get emotional,
maybe I should stop.

One Night in Nam

First thing you know, the light fades
so it's hard to read all those names chiselled on the granite.
All these tourists, they wouldn't
line up, read the names, cry their tears,
now would they? All that suffering flesh,
I'm reminded – it reminds me –
very late one night
in Nam, I see him turn
half-way down the street, and go
through the door, go inside –
no. You know, in this memorial
the fading light
makes a difference
to the long list of names,
makes it hard to find –
he turns, inhales some smoke,
Tiger, that was his name, Tiger Johnson,
then there was a godallmighty flash,
some little kid with blood on her blouse,
gee, it blows you away,
the stain on the wall
and the way the sniper has a bird's
eye view, or a vulture's stare,
looking down out of the sky,
it seems, the bad dream floats
across in front of his eyes
as he peers out of his high window,
Johnson, a bandage on his good arm,
I see him now in the mirror
and that long list of names
written across his reflected face and his golden hair.

Baby Weather

Here comes the baby
walking on his little hands,
ain't that cute?
Then walking on all fours, making forward motion
into some kind of ideogram
like 'Waterfall Pilobolus'
or 'Crane Merchant' which
really means 'Hoochy Kooch in the Alien Lab'.
Hey, come off it, you two
loons! You looked just like one
crazy loon, reading the wind
which was called 'Marvin' or 'Maria'.
I have an unquenchable
thirst, I think. Did I drink enough
or too few six-packs
while you were earning
your fat salary? I see you halt
dead in your tracks
as you tuck down the flaps
of your snow-cap. Did you
know that a snow-storm was
about to come over the hill? You appeared
smiling, as though you were not really there.
An image of you thinks 'he is taking a snapshot again,
a photo of his fellow-man
and his spotted dog.'
Well, that's true. When the
giant rain-burst
caught us unawares
we just hung on and
braced ourselves as we
disappeared into the earth.

Engagement Ring Cycle

I'm sorry; I don't think we've met...
or maybe we did, at the Opera, some other time,
at some distant, earlier time, when one
suffered the onslaughts of the music which one revered
of course, though they say 'Guiseppi Verdi'
is just 'Joe Green' in Italian. Later I'll solve
the Riemann Conjecture, the problem itself
quite loaded with ornate musical motifs
and intimations of the twelve-
tone row, the kind of tune a bird
might sing deep in the forest unheard
except for the faint bird-like prayers
that hardly, barely reach our ears.
That necklace, is that genuine rhine-
stone? It reminds me of an old one of mine.

And so the bloodstained story ends,
the hero dispatches his enemies, and exclaims
to his gathered and astonished friends
that it's now really all over, the weird
King stabbed in his sleep beneath his beard
where his heart is. And as for little me,
it's true, I did have a full-on fling with Maxine
of the Malleable Mandibles. Did you like that scene
where the forest-dwellers crowded together,
greasepaint in thick layers on their faces,
and plunged through the unseasonable mist
and the unlikely freezing weather,
charging back and forth from one end of the stage
to the other? The management can barely afford
that kind of largesse, calls clogging the switchboard.

That one used to be a simple hairdresser,
can you believe? Just like her
to live off her poor long-suffering father
while developing her considerable vocal powers

and dabbling with young men, quite exploitable,
while plowing through her paternal funding,
her boudoir chockablock with various plunder,
including a dress that Zelda wore in *La Loca*, beaded
richly with rubies, her father's pleas unheeded.
They say he made a motza trading Texaco
shares, but he's old now, time to retire.
Each young man finds he can't say no.
She has an economic hold over them
and teases them nightly while a river
of sex keeps their loins on fire.

When it comes to the crunch, what will she say?
Whatever list of excuses she's rehearsed,
heartfelt pleas that attempt to convey
the unsayable, that from the very first
she was a slave to her musical master
and on her flesh he committed every outrage,
gestures quite unacceptable to his wife, a stolid
bourgeoise, sexual attempts in the worst possible
taste, threats and punishments and object lessons
meant to last. Then – his appetites indulged – he dies,
her future opens up, her career reforged,
a new and better-connected Svengali is her sworn
accomplice, soon she's famous and overweight,
then the target of corrosive jealous hate
from the lesser divas, end of story. She cries.

Forget their plotting, piss on them.
Svengali gives you an engagement ring,
look at it glow green and purple and gleam.
Now listen attentively to the sound
of steel cars colliding underground
as James Wright wrote in the 1940s, listening
to the miners mining among their poverty, set
in the slag-heap history of their time, worn to the bone
until they died. No, I don't know who took it,
the gleaming ring, maybe some unknown

gang of men led by Engelbert Nibelheim,
who disappeared with half my jewelry,
they have some hold over me,
and they pull the wool and the scales
over my eyes – shame on me – every time.

So what was the accusation you levelled
at him? What was supposed to be his contribution
to the disaster that blackened your name?
The rippling pectorals and those hefty shoulders
quite wasted: his only role, holding a spear,
a fate that plunged him into a fit of gloom.
Hmmm, those insistent dulcet tones belong
to Detective Vogelsang (or Izzy Fogelsong)
who woke me in the middle of the night
and for hours I tossed and turned, and couldn't fall asleep.
My history will be inscribed on a blue plaque
celebrating the fame that followed my comeback
and the audience will gasp: all their eyes
will be on my fame: see it rise and rise.

The Animal Generation

Seeing the future of the world has been left to us,
just between ourselves,
the previous generation was pretty clumsy.
Always complaining about the rotten wages,
running off into the jungle and staying away
for years. Frankly, I'm sick of them.
Would you wear underwear made of wool?
Their main problem, no humility,
and a strange inability to pay their bills
on time, and their proclivity for telling lies.
Okay, the seasons turn into spring,
I guess there's some kind of continuity
left for us, like how one era
transmutes into another. But what kind of a man
would continually look for shortcuts,
for an easy way to get across the river
saving maybe two hours
and endangering all our lives,
risking everything,
even the future of his very own family?
Okay, here are my conclusions:
a reasonable future has never been found;
we're not qualified to go first.
From now on it's a hand-to-mouth
existence, but in the end you'll be richer
for the experience. When a John Doe
arrives at the morgue, just turn the other cheek.
Empty your wallet, turn out your pockets.
Get used to the grand illusion. Sure, it ain't
much of a holiday – wrong neighborhood –
but hey, it's better than Dachau.

Hateful Mail

'Oh you great whore!' the man
shouted at me. 'All you stupid
creative women are all the same, you all
like lipsticked pigs, you more stupid than
a brainless retiree in a vacation car
at the back of the train, you all so
quick to join the nearest committee
and squeak like some moronic rabbit.
Lady, see what you become,
you write some fuckin stupid poem
and it's just no goddam good,'
cried the horrid man. 'You should be
ashamed of yourself. Now
don't get on your high horse,'
wrote this cretinous blimp –
for his shouting, the ugliest on earth,
was all written out. Paper was his launchpad,
scribble was how he went bonkers and honkers,
foul babble was what ruined
his reputation and his very breath
so that his cough was a horrible hacking
and his tortured ego was an ugly thing, no he was
not a prince of shit, not even
an aristocrat of crap.

My earrings were rhinestones,
and as I walked out into the evening
the flocks of little bats
called out to me, friend to friend.
How can I possibly turn a crazy man into a good
human being, I asked, what are the measures
I must take, what can I do?
Try to write the very best poems
a girl possibly can.

Q and A

Okay, Mister de Mille, I'm ready for my Q and A,
down here in the gloom surrounded by fractions
and fictions and quartets and quintets
at NYU English One Oh One, where I dwelt
for too long, a kind of death watch beetle
in the wainscoting, watching my P's and Q's
and the wagon's panelling – as the earth quaked
and the latest New York Giant of Prose was
stalking about. When I was young I had
a loud, demanding voice. Now I'm voiceless.
No, I don't know where it went.
My students with winter flu went *koph koph koph*,
their ancient Semitic consonants getting better
as the room grew warmer. Maybe it's 'third
time lucky'; and it's true, my last book got much
better reviews. Is that a bullshit detector?
Bring it here! Focus it on that letter:
thanks. Gosh! That fellow-writer! The
ass-hole! Writing one thing, spitting out
another! Lie upon lie, folded
one within the other... to me, a sensitive poet, it
feels like being tortured, like being
waterboarded... or is it 'warboarded'?
Save me, I get things so confused, between the
real and the confected, the living and the dead.

At Arles

Tourists everywhere. Is it rude to stare?
The café table seems to have a tilt
so that my ritual glass of absinthe
tilts too. It's easy being
an art tourist: just bring an easel,
some paints, palette, some canvas...
and please leave your animal
spirits at home. Vincent posed
for a portrait of someone or something
unknown. Boy, that's a difficult
subject. The sunset looks splendid.
Enough absinthe; time I went out
for a walk. Look at them,
buried in history and a tiny room,
around them the blue sky and the night wind –
oh, those stars! One of them staring
at the threatening stars, the other
grimly waiting until the morning
star arrived. Some bread, a piece of cheese,
a flask of wine to help waste the afternoon,
yellow ochre loaded paintbrush in hand
despite the painful coughing
fit. The little calf
at the back of the café is hungry.
It's always hungry.
As for the hungry women,
they are not hungry for hay
but for some other thing, for the promise
of something coloured and splendid.
Vincent carefully opened
his painting kit and saw emptiness
staring up at him: what to
say, what to do about it?
Take lessons in controlling the color-riot.
That's it, paint a black and white dog.
Limit the palette to the light and the dark,
just that, and that's all, he said,

not the yellow light on the window-blind,
and not the little room, the way it
let in the wind and the cruel cold.
My hands are now blistered,
he said, and yours are soft! You
are a stockbroker! Give me my weapon,
this art shit is finished, it is over,
now I shall offer up my body –
the cracking slab of plaster
on the ceiling, the lack of praise,
the stars threatening the evening,
tonight the nerves hunt...

That Greenish Flower

I feel quite sure that I can spell
the name of the greeny Asphodel,
a flower that only grows in hell.

I pondered often how it came
to have such a Greekish name
and such a long, enduring fame.

Perhaps it's the flower Perseus gave
to Philomel, a former slave,
to place upon her father's grave.

I must say, it's a proper bloom
to place upon a father's tomb
to gleam and shine there in the gloom.

But not so rich and not so sweet
as honey-flavoured sausage meat
to place there at your father's feet.

Section Two

Variations on a Theme by E.P. (Elias Pfenning)

An operation, then
braces on a blouse:
How now, round brown cow?

Palpitations, then
a bike cycling down the pike:
ladies' night: mighty nightie show!

This apparition, then
bankers in the cloud:
Bow down, round brown bough.

The Linden Tree

I gobbled a round of Caerphilly, then Theophily
called to me, under the Linden Tree.
Conservatism? Let me count the ways:
Morning suits, grey ties, greys
in every accoutrement, grey imagery
shoaling and fluttering down on me
lost in the grey-green park, under a tree
perhaps, taking the cool morning air
as I lie naked on the grass, bum bare
to the gaze of the policeman, a rare infinity
of arguments circulating deep within me
as the dictates of Theosophy suddenly seem unfair –
am I changing my stance, under the Linden tree?
The work is easy, though the days are tough.
Pray awhile, then that's enough.
Sit with me under the forgiving Linden Tree
and just be.

Young Folly

It must seem like a mountain of folly
to the old people, but we take our chances
and we're always on the ready.

We're on the ready, right now, and yet
they think we're just a troubled handful
of trouble, just can't go straight,

can't go straight like the arrow of time
that speeds from ancient times to right now
to get you between the eyes. This is the realm

behind the eyes, with its whip-quick
answers to how to behave, its cheap vow
to be better, much better, quickly broken

so that what is not better is boarding
at boarding time, those giant flying machines.
We take a drag, and fuck the lung.

Fuck the drag of the air, the horizon's curve.
We're all going on a summer holiday, already gone
into sad age waiting, with just a wave.

The Tyrant Eros

Well, why don't you ask him,
ask him and mask him
already, the hundred fears
that go on for years
and drown us in the weirs
of whatever frightens him

in place of his famous sagacity
and wisdom, oh, him,
let him be just him,
almost
perfect, the ultimate cost
totally lost
without him,

the god of trees,
the god of lawns, just him
who sees
only a person called him
who over-reaches, then he says
let it drift for days
let it drift over countless delays
until the reasons come to him

so that he inaugurates
a time of rare confusion
which reverberates
back and forth, a rare illusion
which lived and then died
until he hid
under one side,
a rare seclusion.

#

Behind his brows
he should simply be
the absence of a house,
the absence of 'could be'
between
what is seldom seen
and what could have been
and what could be,

that is, they
could have striven
to be, to say
what is given,
what could only be
beside a lonely tree
by the sea,
mist driven.

Dog's Life

Come on, time for the exiles
to crow about the lobster bisque
at the Four Seasons, the Come On

at the Seldom Frequent, the bare
back and the naked paws
doing a push-up

in front of the smoosh-up, they
really take the cake, help me, the cloud
in front of the clouded mirror

or the Porche clutch in clutches
thank you, *moi*, palely loitering
near N Lavreinee

that is, North Lavrienee, oh I think
this fucking humidity
will kill me, really, the mud-adobe

huts, the humid softboiled
eggs, that is, me, meaning
thank you,

I have had enough,
good night,
goddam flesh.

The Search

I searched and searched for traces of the love
that was hiding in and around our meeting-place
and then – slowly, regretfully – I read
the thoughts that formed behind your face,

behind your lovely pale blue eyes.
I admit it's hard, I do confess,
to search and search, and not to find
love behind your lovely nakedness.

Your Life

So you wake up at last – welcome to the hereafter –
after your heart attack and the subsequent fall
broke your neck. Dozens of poor people shackled
to their benches, that's the scene, or chained to the walls,
all of them looking snotty and miserable
and shifting their scabby legs in their fetters.
Come on, bright boy, give us a song
as you were wont to do. Now why you suppose
that tall ugly guy is giving you the once-over?
He has just about got you properly figured;
yes, it's the Devil. Think back on your last week
stumbling, alone, wearily up and down Broadway,
middle age weighing on you more and more,
dragging your flabby body and your flabby mood
from skin show to tit show, this is not
teen fun in the back row of the local cinema
with a pretty girl and a bucket of Popcorn Deluxe,
this is the end of old age. You miss the plastic cupholder
and the soda spills on your new car carpet and dribbles away.
This is the point where your old dead father asks
'What have you done with your life?' Your life unrolls
across the floor, it seems pointless now, it is
all vanity. And as for bettering Williams' 'variable foot',
what a waste of time, like your dream of mounting
Miss Blabnik from Rubbermaid… you foul your own nest,
the way you used to shout obscenities at your Mom
on the phone! and the cowardly way you always run
from life's problems, your problems, and the fact that you like
those tacky pictures and the fluorescent light fixtures
that draw the cultural boundaries around your world.
The alarm clock rings in the dreadful hour
when you must carry your hangover into the morning
glare, while you remember some poor guy shitting his pants
as the room fills with cruel laughter:
yes, it's you, that smelly pathetic creature
quite ruined by life's tedious machinery.

Peek-a-boo! The Ol' Debbil can hear you in your house
padding up and down, noting the angles
of the sunlight, carefully, as it comes to rest
on various dusty pieces of furniture, your features
somewhat bloated by your lack of sexual hygiene.
What did you do, with Miss Rubbermaid, last night?
Beside your bed, a half-empty bowl of pretzels,
and a dozen empty bottles on the front stoop.
I don't know how you managed to get along
from day to day, grabbing what's yours
and spitting on what's not, guarding your condition –
selfish alcoholism – and pushing away
the things in the night that peck and claw at you.
Down here in the dark, no more self-deception,
please. Tragic, there's no time left, yet you babble on –
a recital of innocence, good deeds, a sad polyphony
of 'Here, Rover!' 'Good boy!' and whatnot,
it makes us puke, us guilty ones, all of us.
There's a stink of smoke, like an expended cartridge.
'Here you go,' the ugly guy says brightly,
'Guzzle down your last drink: a Rum and Coke!'

Look at my Parents, Will You?

It feels dreadful, when I look in the mirror, when I look
and – ugh! – all I see is a version of my horrible old father.
Is it like that for you? Well, okay, maybe it isn't now,
but wait until you have lived a little, lived wild and free
like me, say, checking out the city, exploring inner space,
until all those drugs that you took hide everything in a fog.
My father was an earth scientist, well, okay, a geologist,
and to me, growing up, he was just like some kind of god.
Not to my mother; she had a different viewpoint. In fact she

hardly managed to get her face on most mornings, she just

sat there trying to get it all on
and all night trying to get it off.

One Variation

Oh, go away, go away!
You are the death of desire,
the way quiet minds
remember and then recall
that hollow feeling of despair,
grey mist, empty streets,
the hollow tread of steps treading down
town, street after street, spring
and fall, winter, snow, mind
after mind, failing then falling now
into an empty house
where a person, all alone.
combs her hair
as we hear the falling rain.

Older than Forty

So now I'm one of these men, older than forty,
men who move slowly and speak softly
and know who they are, but they may not be
quite who they think they are, as they think to

themselves when they pause on the stair-landing,
eyes flicking back and forth, lips moving.
Don't they know every cabin on this ship?
Every plank? Their movements are gentle,

the are surprised to find themselves in mirrors
looking old, looking older, hoping to rediscover –
what was it now? That trick in boy scout lanyard tying
or some other knack, or that other secret

like, for example, how to be their own father.
In the shaving mirror they work at the lather
then shave, then pause – now
while the sun stands still they think of something

they meant to remember – some sound
or some tiny image which holds immense
importance – then they're sliding down the slope
that ends in the green grassy backyard of all those houses.

Man With Banjo

Just sitting under the pines
on a hot day, my banjo
on my knee, just my banjo and me.
Bought me a new conjo
for just me and me,
yes ma'am, I'm a lonesome man.

Maybe we should get together?
Ah, but I have to don my wings,
my special wings, and fly away
to faraway humid Africa,
that jungle which is my home,
don't you know, shadowy Africa
where cries echo through the foetid air,
the jungle mud cries of my Africa
which I call my long-lost home.
In Africa, you won't find any pines,
nor any pine barrens, just heaps of longing
echoing from my banjo and me.

Yes siree, I sure am a lonesome man.
Maybe we should get together
and put on our separate pairs of wings
and fly away...

Me and My Landscape

First, these light coastal winds
swirling and blowing up a little grit,
then a storm, and it becomes violent,
unleashing bright streams and brilliant
rags of cloud and mysterious soot
that always seems to settle on my biography,
a tale of careful lies and untrustworthy travel
that I cunningly inscribe with my left hand.
Enough of this metaphorical topography!
Dive, deep, into this human geography!

So: it's true, I always seem to seek
some crack in the heavens, a sign
in the clouds, a rent in the sky the color
of lime-yellow quartz, just for me, or citrine.
I like citrine. This trail of smoke persists
across the pale blue. My point of entry
is to turn my landscape into a mode of speech
where the words build a second landscape where I might meet
King Arthur surrounded by all his pageantry,
prince of poverty, 'king of a rainy country',

nonetheless a landscape full of a strange beauty
where a sky the colour of the blade of a knife
holds back its rain, or brings forth
a flother of snow, where a bank of cloud is
speaking to me, resting on a solid column of air.
And in this delicate language an ampersand
says there's more to come, adventures just for me on
the agenda, in my personal sky a sign –
a flash of citrine – and below the horizon and
off to one side a slab of sand

that makes a beach ruffled by a blue wind
where a particular armoured ghost
drags his chains, and in the sand molecular
quartz glitters, and a metallic silicon scent

imbues the landscape with a strange smell –
ah, imbues... or is it an incomprehensible shape?
Time will tell – a rainy landscape of which
I am the sole, only and lonely inhabitant.
I accept gladly that there will be no escape
from my home, my unconscious country, my landscape.

Et in California Ego

Last week, I knew it was time to leave the city.
The way the sun glinted off window-panes, a warning
arriving on my front lawn with the morning
newspaper, and the shape of that funny cloud...
and those kids breaking stuff, it shouldn't be allowed
one time, let alone — the way it is now — twice.
No, man, it's definitely not pleasant, not nice.
So I packed and got the hell out of this shitty

place, filled the tank, beat it. Hey, it ain't funny,
the way peculiar things kind of happen
in their odd way, how certain envelopes fall open
at the fatal news, the way your best friends just leave
and abandon you to your career, and you grieve
pointlessly. The Sheriff swings that rawhide goad,
and you take off down that dusty road.
Hey, do you have enough money?

Yes, honey... you turn to look back, but instead
the future appears before you, every day
longer than the last, your dog... say,
was that your dog Hobo disappearing behind that row
of tents? Then a male voice on the radio
speaks a special message just for you, and between
one gas station and the next, that pale green
landscape just grows darker, the blue thread

crawls behind your dawdling ballpoint on the map
as you plot your escape from the horrid Barbary Coast
to that new place, where you can honestly boast
of your massive talent turning out column after column
of prose as mellifluous and convincing as it was solemn,
read by senior executives and beatniks in cafés
along with the morning news of various calamities. Graze
peacefully there, half snoring, your lap-

top snapped shut, but the road begins to wind
higher into the hills, the hairpin bends and turns
causing the brakes to heat up as the rubber burns

from your squealling tires, your fingers crossed
as you check the map and hope you're not lost,
not in these unspeakable badlands, not just here
where the good things fade into a pale mist, where
you realise you're lost, and you think you'll never find

your way home: time to stop and park
in this trailer park, yes, it's late
with a bad moon rising, with the endless wait
until dawn — don't nod off! — then you unpack
your flimsies, don pajamas, snooze in back
until you're woken by the unbearable light of a star
gleaming and glimmering through the trees, as far
from earth as you are from your home, the dark

seeming to grow around you, the clouds to loom
over all the sky, dark now, your cries
feeble and fading over the low rise
ahead, now a train loaded with mounds of coal
pulls by, steel wheels on steel tracks roll
onward and upward, you hear the whistle sing
its mournful song, plucking the single string
of your heart, the low smoke plume

or maybe it's a locomotive plume of steam
lit from below by a fitful boiler flame.
You know your life ahead of you is just the same
as everything you've left behind, the endless night
concealing the world, but then the unbearable light
of the sun does too, with its immense
and world-bestriding blinding indifference —
and, waking, you trudge ahead with your dream.

To keep going demands an awful effort of will.
You know that what you believe is just not natural.
Your life seems like a rusting, failed factory
that tries to manufacture little pieces of sky
but instead makes more dark clouds. You long for release
from that pressure to flee the horror, to find peace.
In the mirror no monster, just a girl who looks pretty.
Start the motor. No more self-pity.

In Plato's Bed

In the middle of the earthquake when the wall begins to cave-
in, when the floors and the goddam wall
quake and shatter and move towards the broken window
with glass everywhere, before too long
you begin to hear a sour grinding
noise, as someone unwraps the rain-wet tarpaulin
from the back of the truck and the secret diagram
begins to unravel between the sudden sound of the 'chop
chop' and the cry of 'Who's the goddam Chink
with the meat cleaver and the unlit cigarette,
huh?' widely and generously bestowed
on one and all, the halt and the lame, upon
all who came here in the middle of the night, with the patience
able to range across the stretch of egregious capital
from the blind fumbling bodies unto the very seeing eyes
who were able to see right through to the loose
shifts and the drenched people under the waterfalls
as the soaked bodies grew nearer and nearer
and spoke to us even more gently and softly
about the upholstery torment of a particular chair
and the painful pallid reflections in the silvered mirror
while the bitter winter wind hummed and whistled
around the corners and the tiles, so slick and wet,
in just such a manner, speaking English, so
did the Great Greek Plato deny the baseless rumours
spread by his enemies, stories of long and pointless travail,
fruitless research into trigonometry and architecture, beginning
at the start and going on and on, once again
innocent and revelling in the new-born status of the unforgiven.

Show Us at the Ming Place

It happened when I was about seventeen.
I wanted to write a story or maybe a poem.
At least, that's what I thought
at the time, and about then I shat
my pants, jeesh! what a comedown! since
then I have hardly been able to buy a drink at the bar,
you know, one of those pastel sweet fizzy ones
you buy for your girl friend or maybe a funny puppy,
you buy one drink or maybe two
and right then it happened,
you began to write a real poem,
one that said
in terrifying language 'she laughed
and she moved so beautifully', or so I thought
at the time, it's just what you do
to move forward the plot, the painfully articulated plot,
the lot of love's strangely located and odd game
that no one understands until much much later
when everything has gone wrong, and mid-number
you pause and you stumble and you stand
in the middle of the jazz pause while the band's personnel
pause, dazed and amazed, some right off and some right on.

Meditation at Breakfast

You want to meditate on a what? No, that's not possible.
Maybe tomorrow, you can meditate on it, maybe the day
after tomorrow. You know, the angry way you
shout when you think you're alone in the kitchen,
that's not a good sign. Meditate on a basketball?
Are you serious? Come on, have a little breakfast
and cheer yourself up. Right now you look like a husk
of your former self. I just know, that's all. Jojoba oil,
it's good for the skin, you massage it into the pores,
then wipe it all off, then rub in a little granulated pepper —
okay, hold the pepper — then macerate a little 'Heart's-Ease'
in warm vinegar — it's a herb, good for the complexion — just in case
you need it. Talking of breakfast, or rather, of 'breaking
fast', there's no need to behave like a monastic monk in his cell.
Go ahead, grab yourself some bacon, a whole piece,
not just a snippet! Go ahead, fill your bowl
right up with muesli and oats and grains and some whole
wheat things, grab a grapefruit with its wrinkly skin
covered in pockmarks, they're mainly pleasant to eat,
a little sour, maybe, but the pink-fleshed ones are often sweet.
Now Kevin, I think it's time we talked a little about discipline.
You know here at the Meditation Center we're mainly devout
Buddhists or at least pantheists, having come to our senses
about the problem of meditating on the general emptiness

that people — Kevin? — people generally find within
themselves — Kevin? Are you listening? Within or maybe without...

Coffee at the Palace of the Great Hoon

hoon /huːn/ *Austral./NZ informal; noun: a lout or hooligan,*
        especially a young man who drives recklessly. The whole
        family was wiped out because some drunken hoon had to
        drive his car. *ORIGIN 1930s: of unknown origin.*

His beard tangled around his shanks as he descended
The rain-wet stairs, and from the garden a macaw called
In a red tongue. There were two of me, I was beside myself
As I helped untangle the Great Hoon's beard.
'Shall I speak?' spake the Great Hoon. 'Oh, I'm all ears,'
I replied. Spittle everywhere. Jewels here and there
Scattered on the gleaming stone, opals rained
On the glowing marble, and I thought I heard
Between the Parrot's paragraphs of speech, a distant sea
Murmuring on a granulated strand, and thought I saw
Among the glittering foliage, in the mirror of myself,
The Gaudy Hoon made immeasurably strange.

Tomb in the Rain

There's shelter from the rain, under this ledge.
So who is this novelist, to grandly bequeath
his talent to me? I have sat and watched
till the sun set, and all is obscured,

until all that's left is the sound of bells
from the distant church, and at my back
a slab of stone bearing a strange hieroglyph,
a carving of a great whale and writhing eels and shells

that squirm and wreathe under the moonlight and coil
from air to sea and back again, all unreconciled
to the high horrid gods behind the salty altars
and the broad purple plain of the stars

high above all, that glimmer and somehow contrive
to glint on the wavetops and shallows and steeps
of the waves, that punish this old-time mariner
so that the more he dreams, the more he sleeps.

Fly

Yep, it's the witching hour
when you're never quite sure
whether I am about to tell a lie —
no wonder you don't feel secure.

This colour, or that? I just chose
according to whim, no more
to it than that, blink of an eye
and it's over, the easy rapport

between the "f" and the "i", the ligature
that holds us apart or together, that tore
from your throat a muffled cry
that I had not heard before,

so much so that I swore
as my head bounced off the floor
and in my eye pieces of sky
spun about, my head was sore

for hours, well, three or four
hours, who cares what you wore
as you made your final reply:
don't talk to the bore no more,

say bye to the old school tie
as you leave, closing the door.

Section Three

Cold Spring

All the sorrows of Miles Wilson's
loutish adolescence were redeemed
at seventeen, in 1944, when he
fell in love with trucks.
'What's the matter with your coat, dear?'
And Sam knew he wouldn't hear
anything prettier than that all summer.
A few of the girls were crying as they
helped to swell the long, cheering ovation,
and young Sally climbed up on the platform
to embrace him and press her face
against his sweated shirt.
You're going to be a man.

Power

Mr Wilson went out to look for his gas cylinder,
into the blazing Spanish sun and the dust.
Anyone can tell you're a man of education.
It was, of course, the end, but at the same time
you had to be prepared for everything,
even escape. 'Bastards,' the man said,
and his hand lay wearily where it had got to,
over his heart; he imitated the prudish attitude
of a female statue, one hand over the breast
and one upon the stomach.
But the boy had already swung the door open
and put his lips to his hand
before the other could give himself a name.

Quiet

After dinner I sat and waited for Thompson
in my room over the rue Catinat; he had said
'I'll be with you at latest by ten,' and when
midnight struck I couldn't stay quiet any longer
and went down into the street.
'We've made it,' Thompson said, and even in my pain
I wondered what we'd made: for me, old age,
an editor's chair, loneliness; and as for him,
I know now that he spoke prematurely.
Should I invite my saviour to dinner,
I sometimes wondered, or should I
suggest a meeting for a drink
in the bar of the Continental?
I tried not to think of all the pipes I had smoked
at home. Everything had gone right with me
since he had died, but how I wished
there existed someone to whom
I could say that I was sorry.

Heaven

I met Sally Williams for the first time
in more than half a century
at my mother's funeral. I suppose
the authorities lost interest
when the diamond robberies started.
The names sound so oddly like those of horses.
The man with the rabbit nose went twitching by,
grey as the grey morning. There is, of course,
a considerable difference in our ages,
but she is a gentle and obedient child,
and often in the warm scented evenings
we read Browning together: 'God's in his heaven –
all's right with the world.'

The Rats

There is a sense in which any good biography
appears a lucky accident. But Smith had made
no mark: the world had stamped him, not he
the world: no rolling stone gathered less moss.
The opening of the year 19-- found him still
enjoying the novel experience of a regular income;
for his case still hung fire, and his allowance
continued. 'If I stay anchored near an island,
I must keep continually awake;
for, the moment I cease moving,
I am invaded my swarms of swimming rats,
who in the winter are so voracious that they
attack even the man who is motionless.' Hail,
strange tormented spirit, in whatever
hell or heaven has been allotted
for your everlasting rest.

Honor

Doctor Anderson stood on the old
wooden wharf on the Delaware,
among the rails and yellow cranes, watching
where a horizontal plume of smoke stretched
over the New Jersey Pine Barrens. Old men
are not very demanding, or so they say,
and girls like that are glad of a rest.

Father Kennedy looked up at him
with the inflamed eyes of a dog
who defends a bone. He swung his good leg
out of the bed and reached for the crutch.

He realised that never before had she been
so close to him as she was now.

Variations and Reverse Mazurka

*employing a form devised by John Keats and
beginning with a line by Kenneth Koch*

This Connecticut landscape would have pleased Vermeer –
Canal, broken streetlight, weedy drain.
The way the colored pennants flicker in the air
Around the used car lot, and Lovers' Lane
Gloomy under the willows, littered with sticky
Spent balloons and empty jugs of wine,
The sound of bodies bumping in a car.
    It ain't Delft – be picky,
Go on, complain. *I hate America.* Fine.
    Capitalism has travelled very far.

This snapshot would have been liked by Leonardo –
If only he hadn't been a total shit –
The trailer trash poster of Brigitte Bardot
Semi-nude – they like a bit of tit.
To make a real impression on the trade –
It's difficult, when you're mostly pissed.
Who is this Dago with his look of gloom?
    To climb the slippery grade,
It isn't easy, when you've slit your wrist.
    So curse Connecticut and get your broom.

This Texas vista would have tickled Titian –
More than that last one, in the Carolinas:
The morning light turning almost Grecian,
And then the debacle of ten drunken miners
In a blasted landscape of rock and coal
And dirty starving children – no thanks.
In Dallas the citizens felt that art was good:
    classy, on the whole,
So culture, restaurants, and drive-in banks
    All helped to polish up a neighbourhood.

This Iowa cornfield would have seemed like fun
To Renoir, as the crop-dusting plane turned
To make another deadly strafing run
At actor Cary Grant who had hardly earned
Such animosity – real name Archie Leach,
His accent fading year by US year,
His English manner growing more urbane,
    Tanning on a beach –
His features now showing a touch of fear
    As he flees the bullet-spitting plane.

This wintry prospect would have blissed out Bacon,
The icy road, the sodden banks of snow,
The postcard views of toy-like Interlaken
Where tourists with their skis are wont to go.
While Rubens, rattled, would have shut the door,
Their antics on the slopes diverted Degas,
Though their wealth would have vexed van Gogh,
    Who much preferred the poor.
And Andy Warhol, drinking in a gay bar,
    Watched the crowded dance-floor ebb and flow.

Turner would have endorsed this watery sight:
The *Andrea Doria* emerging from the fog
Off North America. She should have turned right,
But turned left, says the ship's log.
Impaled by a Swedish boat, the *Stockholm*. The mystery:
Both had radar. Sixteen hundred survived.
Steely Dan, earning another dollar,
    wrote them into history.
Useless facts: among those alive,
    Cary Grant's wife, and Mike Stoller.

This lurid landscape would have bothered Braque:
The crowds, the traffic, and the noise.
He knocks back a shot of Cutty Sark
And takes another look: girly boys,
Huge videos blathering, Times Square
Crawling with junkies and emaciated hookers.

On the street the people come and go
    Taking the polluted air,
Some malformed, some real lookers –
    There's Michael and his buddy Angelo!

This Alabama airport would have bemused
Walt Disney and his team of animators.
They'd admire the planes, buy some booze,
and photograph the handsome aviators.
Look, whole families shopping (in the mall)
(Ginsberg), children putting on weight,
Passengers arriving and departing on time –
    Spring, Summer, Fall...
Well, some early, and a few late,
    But it all works, turning on a dime.

Five Egyptian Pieces

Alexandria

Think of the village baby.
A scene of adventure – the dream of Europe.
The eyes of marching armies fostered perplexity
that marred all its books and intellectuals
and opened their minds to the encyclopaedia of algebra
and carmine bear remembrances.
The tumult of the bears has maintained the fear.

Cairo

Ladies choose a country to call symbolic,
uncertain of which temptation to desire,
the theatre of maiming, the pain,
the poets, the verses frozen,
aware of the men and women of this road,
the cradle impossible to forget: our origins.
The Mediterranean exploits of Herodotus
spread to both of the memory vaults.
The stone murmurs our common heritage.

Giza

We know the imagination of letters,
the country of hanging gardens, this
speaks to us. We are bound by its women,
children play with hope. The transparent work
without play is reported missing.
The expert should like food.
Ladies are prepared to become rich
despite the clangour of morality.

Luxor

In our shelter, harm depends on a fresh chance
for decadence. We have toyed with nostalgia,
and vengeance is a blind alley.
Am I not ancient? We wish to spread
a host of luxuriant factors for play.

We need her rich experience and feelings of despair.
It intensifies the suffering.
There has never been such abomination.
Each road must be ripe for the sad future,
embracing water and the thirst for travel.

Thebes

The joint will lend an ear
to the consciousness.
It would lag behind concrete,
for the sad future is embracing water
and the thirst for travel.

Act, think about the pool, these fields.
Relax: go further to the shore,
create a stimulant for our partners.
A high-level personality means breathing.
Our neighbours must be separated.

Least Said

The ice-cream headache has you seeing double
as Goody Twoshoes calls by your table to arrange
some kind of smooth-talk conference full of limitless
possibilities, lots of cocktails, two naked men and naturally
behind the pot-plant your mother throwing up
as she always does, come midnight. Some aperçu! Excuse me, I
have to go... Look, I didn't really mean to say 'naturally' –
that was a Freudian slip, which misbehaviour has increased
among the dilettante young. There, there,
wipe your eyes, sweetheart, and stop rubbing
your bald patch. Ugh! The store detective wants to grill
your mother about the missing underwear... or so he said.

'Life, like a dome of many-coloured glass,' Shelley said,
'stains the white underpants of eternity.' Radiance, whatever. Same
difference: like how Joy H. Breshan makes up a singular constituency,
your twin sister: belie, beleaguer, belabour the point, belike.

Manacles

I was born with a silver ribbon in my hair,
a fizzing link to the aether that compels me to
listen to the sky babbling. I broke there,
and came back a different creature.
Pity me – no, go to hell – he lays bare
trails of financial ruin as indeed he had to,
was told to, his face with farinaceous powder
a poltergeist in the gloomy room,
audience supplied – back of the college – my life
worth a dime if you're lucky and fool around
this dilemma banging from the world-deafened ears,
from heaven sent down to poison earth.

Sit and doodle, that's how it's done?
The driver laughed then cranked the volume,
then audio imperative mood: tower taller,
high power bracket racket: and I heard
one listening to the others –
crumpled linen tableaux, blue horizon,
the detective ponders why the dog
didn't bark – because he refused
he was refused, motto: 'garbage in, garbage out',
because nil bullshit, nil bullshit:
ten electronic eyes in the cafeteria
that scan the bar code key and judge you.
Sadness separates the sheep from the night,
to endure in order to fill out the plot,
to find out about the others finding out, and boys –
jazz, dark liquor, the bones around the brain,

write 'We were born into the secrets of Gomorrah
Under the Sign of the Double Key' –
that is, lock slot metal type reversing mirror
nihil obstat, determined to learn it quick
under the humming sign

#

of the Great Reader above and behind
the edge of the observable universe.
Now he remembers his dad
working on a lamp, but I guess someone will
be at the park entrance offices – those
sheep in the photo must all die, watch the gas.
Mom stayed in a hotel, listened to the radio,
the tiny yellow diamonds – gift
from the princess – spilled on the lounge seat.
In the kitchen, a family growing old,
that is, time made flesh,

lover made into stranger, here
in this bright garden, or
you squatting on the roof or nodding
on the rear seat, this one summer night
will never come again – Dear Blotto –
just this once you didn't make it,
your lucky win was timed to come
long ago, when dazed and panting
in the middle of the party everything appeared
part of a plot – the weather speaking miserably,
pointing up the lovely colours of his tie
and to you in an empty stone chapel
a full-blown devil of the ink-well
rose up and babbled and looked around –
advising you to cheat and bribe, and why
the theories are wet with bracket creep is up to you,

Carolyn whispered I've spent a weekend –
camping officer name's erased, he said they seem
plausible, they also murmured luminous surface
within a dirty magazine, women live there
a lovely young sprig of possibilities, in
hope arrayed. I'm Doctor Incognito
here in hospital, victim shot through,

#

more trouble, the Greek Coast and its
rotten weather, cottages packed with
bedroom ardour – so they'd developed
other tickets – it was here in the underground
she'd stare at her hands, fearful of a stranger
and the messages he brought from her
childhood, wrapped in tissue paper
and scented with summer heat, a little good
forbids the nameless feelings in my throat.

Rubies

Glow White and the Three Dwarfs Remaining –
Sneezy, Sleazy and Greasy: we were just
guys together, once, digging up diamonds, pals –
then this whirlwind of womanhood
descended on us out of the forest
with her perfume, her mystery and her periods.
She owned this Summer Retreat – Gnome, Alaska –
perched on a mountain covered with glittery gneiss
and a pool that nobody swam in. Or
so she said: who could tell? Then
her winter home in the Republic of Ireland,
tax, natch. We were just rubes della bosco,
hicks and hayseeds with a stash of gems,
blokey yokels with a thuggish charm,
or so she'd have us believe. What happened
to the other four? No one can remember.
Nodding off among the gloomy furniture.
She's gone again, with that Lothario,
to 'liquidate' a sack of rubies in Lausanne.
Tell us again, Sleazy, the one about
Sleepy and the Doc, the good old days,
before things changed, and we got to be rich.

Four Variations on a poem by Pam Brown

Pam Brown
Eyes on Potatoes (part two of eight)

downloading Laurie's poems,
pages flutter off the printer tray
and get mixed-up with bits of Bolton's.
I walk out to look up at the vast sky
lit by a huge full moon   the night
is tranquil   everyone's indoors watching
crap tv   the muffled sounds of soaps
lulled by wintry fossil fuels and
natural gas,   sleepy dwellers lounge tonight,
cooking aromas on this side of the building
aren't nearly as good as Stella's
smoky herring and pirozhki   on the opposite

Sweet Potato Sonnet, 1

Downloading Larry Sawyer's verse,
And printing them, pages fall to the floor
And get mixed with bits of the broken door.
I look up to see a vast spectral nurse
Lit by a flashlight, glint of needle in hand.
I wish, you read this, the needle drops.
Outside, the muffled tread of cops
Dazed by a few chilled ales and
Dashboard radio, groovers' lounge tonight,
Doing their rounds, no one has died,
Inhaling – is it tobacco? No? – smoke,
Chewing on a roll-mop herring, flashlight
Again, and now on the opposite side
Of the planet a poet takes a toke.

2

Downloading ancient Horrie's tales –
Horrie the Wog Dog (Ian Idriess), then
Pages flutter off the printer tray when
Verses are mixed with torn bits of sails.
I walk out to look up at the huge sky
Lit by a normal-sized moon, night
Is dozey, pals watching crap 'Flight
Of the Condor' on TV, muffled cry
Strangled by open wood fires and smoke,
Sleepy fellers drift and dream now,
Cooks dream like a dozing cow,
A Jersey, smiling like a good bloke,
Not as mysterious as Stella's romance
With Colonel Pirozhki of the Russian Dance.

3

Uploading Harry's poems, Harry Reade,
Antedilulvian commo, decent bloke,
They say, Aussie Cuban Battler, take a toke,
One day Sydney, next a manly deed
With Castro's rebel army, sure,
Join the left-wing push and march away
As pages flutter from the printer tray
And gather on the lino kitchen floor.
I walk out to look up at the vast sky
lit by a full moon: the failing night
is tranquil, friends watching fright
TV, shots, groans, muffled sigh.
Here in the mountains, warmed by fuel,
We are our own ghosts, sparkling like a jewel.

4

Downloading poems and bits of errant pose,
Pages flutter out of the printer bin
And get mixed-up with bits of human skin.
I wander and look up at the vast sea of prose
Lit by a dead moon, the trembling night
is wavering, friends indoors gazing
Dumb at the TV, wobbly screen blazing
Pointless messages so we get a fright.
Is the gas natural? Or is it late?
Cooking aromas tell us it's all right,
nearly as good as Stella's golden light
Illuminating a herring on the plate
Where the gustatory thrill is on the button,
Tasting like a lazy heap of mutton.

Adjectivitis at Lagunitas

All the adjective thinking is about loss.
In this it resembles all the adjective thinking.
The idea, for example, that each particular erases
the adjective clarity of an adjective idea. That the adjective-
faced adjectivepecker probing the adjective adjective trunk
of that adjective birch is, by his presence,
some adjective falling off from an adjective world
of adjective light. What did that mean? Or the adjective notion that,
because there is in this world no one thing
to which the bramble of adjectiveberry corresponds,
a word is elegy to what it signifies. What did that mean?
We talked about it late last night and in the voice
of my friend, there was an adjective wire of grief, a tone
almost adjectival. What did that mean? I understood that
talking this way, everything dissolves: justice,
pine, hair, woman, you and I. Dissolves? There was a woman
I made love to and I remembered how, holding
her adjective shoulders in my hands sometimes,
I felt an adjective wonder at her presence
like a thirst for salt (what did that mean?), for my adjective river
with its adjective willows, adjective music from the adjective boat,
adjective places where we caught the adjective adjective-adjective fish
called adjectiveseed. It hardly had to do with her.
Longing, we say, because desire is full
of adjective distances. I must have been the same to her.
But I remember so much, the way her hands dismantled bread,
the thing her father said that hurt her, what
she dreamed. Okay, I remember only three things.
There are moments when the career trajectory of a poet is as adjectival
as words, days that are the adjective flesh continuing. What did
that mean? Such tender ambition, those afternoons and evenings,
saying adjective, adjective, adjective.

Loxodrome

Jet lag at four a.m. in Manhattan, a little snow outside,
making a pure dream out of dirty streets the way
a dash of verse makes a cultural space out of rumination, or
the way a splash of vermouth transforms cheap gin
into something interesting.

Last night in a busy restaurant on the outskirts of Tokyo
my hamburger was accompanied to perfection
by a light French red, something from Languedoc
a troubadour might have approved.

Maybe – ensconced in the heart of capital – I should compose
a 'Letter to a Lady' in the mode of Pope or perhaps
'A Letter to a 72
' in the mode of Auden, seeing as
how he was a New Yorker, more or less,
to excavate and then explain how the Empire
cast a gladiator's net over the world of discourse in English,
with by preference American spelling
as it is closer to the Latin, where a coloratura
is honored in her labors by a practical nation
and where individuality and aggression go hand in hand.

No, perhaps a model like Ken Bolton's lecture 'Untimely
Meditations' read at the *The Space of Poetry* conference,
a forgiving model which would require an attention to
indentation (the putting in of teeth),
where Les Murray is branded the Bad Fairy
of Australian Poetry, hexing lesser talents
to a life of sweeping cinders from the hearth of verse.
On my last visit to the Bad Apple I noticed
from the bus the PARK LANE LIQUOR STORE,
where I must pay proper homage and
buy a bottle of Strega for a friend
in honor of O'Hara's take on New York,
an out-of-towner's enthusiasm that Gilbert Sorrentino
looks down upon, he being stamped out in Brooklyn
by the very machine those rubes from Boston
were in awe of: New York in its garments of horrible power.

#

I should have said *looked* down upon, past tense: he died
after I wrote that line, before I wrote this one.
Last night, thirty thousand feet above Alaska
I invented the theory of Marsupial Poetry which justifies,
by a cruel inversion, that power: where
Darwin rules, red in tooth and claw, only
the fittest survive and prosper – though poets
hardly breed poets, and fight off young pretenders in a flurry
of anxiety that would block the passing-on
of traits for survival.

Five a.m.: twenty yellow cabs cruising Second Avenue
in a southerly direction: friendly sharks
or a New York School of Transport Alternatives
clocking on before dawn, the store awnings dusted
with powder snow. But then, in the background
of my musing: Columbo's kangaroo.

An alternative, by way of light relief, or a change
as good as a holiday, from the drudgery of verse
that herds its bovine metaphors across the range
of literature, where rhyme is the very curse
that heals and liberates. What I mean is
what I write, is what I mean, in three layers:
the rococo work with its complex and tricky engines,
the musing upon the teleology of such a work, and
the view from a high window of that culture, its stratagems,
the subtle woven pattern with its many meanings,
its much-rehearsed and pointless vanity.
A letter to the *New Yorker*, addressed to
the successful Man of Letters: dear
Better Self: when you're sick of the infighting,
boasting and general shit that make up the life
of a literary fellow, take a trip Down There and relax
among the marsupials. You'd die of what? Boredom?
A stiff black coffee with a dash of brandy
and a plate of eggs Benedict Arnold – *traître d'oeufs* –
and a look through those old books that no one
reads any more, but when I look up, the sunset
says something lurid against a shop window,
reminding me of John Forbes and the way ephedrine

lends a glow to the everyday, in his highly-colored world,
the nitty-gritty quiddity and the banal,
and if you capture that glow and bottle it
you have something to build on, maybe even a career.

Like the night I read with John and Peter Schjeldahl
at the Harold Park Hotel, to a crowd of five hundred
who loved it all – 'I've always wanted to know
what it felt like to be a rock star, and now, thanks to you,
I do!' Schjeldahl said to my wife, and Forbes for once
didn't make some hurtful remark about how successful
other people were, and the bar stayed open till late...
and as I clean the pool that Forbes never saw, I imagine
Ken Bolton watching over the fence – *over there, John,*
you missed a leaf! – it all falls into place, then
dissolves into dreck before I can write it down
like that dream I had once on Mandrax that meant so much
and melted into drivel in the sunlight.

Back in Sydney I meet a friend at Canteen
and the cute waitress ignores me again. My heart
is in my pocket, it's an old book of Ashbery's,
when his work was young and sweet –
and when I drive into town I think of it,
how there was a time once when the lyric
could be fitted to America, but alas no more, only
gothic horror fits – from Henry James to Stephen King –
waiting at the lights I notice, far off and high up,
a life-size model of a man on a charger, on top of a building,
waving a heraldic banner twenty stories above Sydney
against a sky smudged with smoke, representing
something noble about aspiration and capital,
but too high up to be 'readable' in the advertising agency
sense of the word, like Poulenc, or Mallarmé, say, or even
Rimbaud who was a talented and ambitious shit like
some people we know, but with a few extras:
prize-winning Latin, a tank full of talent
and a future as big as the twentieth century.

#

Refreshment break: Sir Francis Bacon and Charlie Parker
had one thing in common: they stopped for a chicken.
It killed Bacon, and at the start of Parker's career
may have seemed a sign. Sigmund Freud and
Arthur Hugh Clough both applied for jobs in Australia,
and were knocked back. Then, when you think about it,
Clough and Cartier-Bresson had one thing in common:
they were the ambitious sons of rich cotton merchants.
The machinery of Arthur Hugh Clough's hexameters
strikes us like a tireless mechanical rocking horse
galloping evenly over the heather. The rhythm is
soothing and slightly narcotic. Once you have the key,
history opens up like a can of sardines. The air
has become dry and cold, like the air over Washington,
where the splash of scattered dogwood blossoms
lightens the gloom under the trees in the spring.

If I wished hard enough, would John Forbes come back?
He did in my dreams, but only to rectify a minor
error of mine, and now I have forgotten what it was;
a clumsy gesture in the Romantic mode,
or perhaps asking for more, like
Oliver Twist at the trough of verse? Or maybe
just being clever but not clever enough,
or far too sincere when sincerity comes
in scare quotes and wearing jeans
carefully not ironed but bleached in irony.

Abjure

There were some words he swore to abjure
In future – *abjure*, for one, *ineluctably*,
Suddenly – 'suddenly there was a flash of lightning' –
They hardly let you know they're coming – *saintly*,
As in 'saintly motorcyclists' (Ginsberg),
Persiflage – a bon mot of professors – *bon mot* also,
Celebrity, as in 'he was a Hollywood celebrity',
Nonce-words like *smalling* – 'the whole fabric
Smalling into distance' – *quark*, and several
Hapax legomena including *flother.*
He switched off his computer and gazed out
At the expensive suburb, and the Aston Martin.
That felt better: from now on his
TV ads would have the purity of a Proust.

Opus Plus

Opus plus comment:
Click the metal button –
Second thoughts: press your
Fleshy lips against the
Elevator button that will lift you
Up to Paradise, your haircut
A broken promise you
Forgot to cash. Gasp out a
Spiel at the cash register,
Lobbying your hobby
As a cascade of bets
Flushes the plate glass
And washes your wishes
Down the drain.

Poem Beginning With a Line by Bunting

Boasts time mocks cumber Rome.
Roasts thyme scents set on ledge.
Ghosts rhyme under Wren's dome.
Stone gives axe sharper edge.
Anger, pride, youth are slowly spent.
Pound disposes, humans merely err.
Plain prose is spoken like a gent,
But verse stirs up Northern burr.
Spy for MI6 and Anglo Oil
Stirring up trouble in Tehran.
Home at last. Brag, tenor bull.
Every brag attracts another fan.
Bye, Basil Bunting, meet your God.
Poet now rests beneath the sod.

The Year my Shadow Pagoda Lost its Savage Home

'Never use these words in a title.' – Pam Brown

There were harmless little words like 'pagoda',
Words like tiny orange birds, that were best
Not thought of. But my Imaginary Pagoda,
My many-tiered temple, or maybe –
Hard to tell – my ornamental imitation of one,
Promising Heaven but never delivering – yes,
I know people like that – it vanished one day,
Having lost its savage home in the jungle
And the respect of the local cigarette-smokers.
Archaeologists and Anthropologists flocked there,
With questions about their beliefs, it was a miracle
And a paradise to them, the natives untouched
By paradoxical Western values, only Eastern corruption
With its usefulness and its dark unsung heroes.

The Hairdresser

Big Al had broken jail and was on the loose.
Fellow had a liking to assault and batter,
That's what put him in the calaboose.
Now he's free to roam and blab and natter,
To go hungry, explore the scrub, chatter
To a hairdresser he met at midnight – the town's one
Street silent, save for the distant clatter
Of a goods train on a country run.
Moonlight. Philosophy. A laugh, a shot of rum.
What was this guy doing in his pyjamas,
Drunk, wandering late at night, done
With cutting hair for the wives of dopey farmers?
Al mused: give up trouble? Blend
Into the human race? Not bloody likely, in the end.

The Love Song of J. Edgar Hoover

Punish me with jugs of honey
Tie me down with bramble twine,
Stuff my mouth with wads of money –
        Please be mine.
Kick me with your winklepickers,
Gag me with your wrinkled knickers,
Make me lick your brutal shoe:
        Love me do.
Garnish me with couch and fescue,
Dress me in an acid dressing,
Telegram your roughest blessing,
Be my howling search and rescue –
When I'm lost and all alone,
        Take me home.

Poem Beginning with a line by John Anderson

It is the time of clarity, noon,
When one creature recognises another.
A banker sees a policeman as his brother.
A street sweeper leans against his broom.
The ants are my friends, also a rabbit.
The Jindyworobaks come to mind.
No European models – they're unkind,
And plunge us into war; horrible habit.
But our language comes from Europe: Latin,
Greek, Germanic, Indo-European roots.
In the pre-dawn chill, magic things happen.
An animal that never reads books eats boots
And leaves quickly. Dawn breeze, leaves
Fall. Cut wheat stands in sheaves.

Postcard From Ischia

Time to pen another postcard from Ischia.
News? In the surf, blue plastic foam,
Not much else to report. I'm feeling friskier
Than I used to: in Italy you can roam
From one pizzeria to another, pleasantly dizzy
With espresso after espresso, feeling fizzy,
An old goat on Goat Island – no,
Different continent, memory mixup, don't go.
Seniors' Cruise at last, recall failing
On the beach – Capri – off Italy, drat,
Here I am in the snapshot, floppy hat,
Getting ready with rich friends to go sailing –
Not like Shelley, great poet, wed
To the deep, drowned in Paradise, dead.

Hark

Liberals rake it in. Yawn: an awesome nap.
A long line of cars crept along Baghdad roads.
Horror night... There's one... got him! Crap!
Declining performances across the board.
'It changed my whole life,' he wrote. 'Toads
Are just misunderstood frogs.' Strange:
The senior officers wanted to discover the Lord.
Children fix errors on their phone screens.
The kids see it, and it's making cultural change.
Even in their middle age, they seemed like paint
Drying on a wall. Kids eating baked beans.
Mertz was Mawson's companion, who died of fear.
Mertz was one of the most popular writers, a saint.
That was the biggest load of shit you'll ever hear.

The Creature

I remember an English composition teacher –
Classroom hours filched from chores on the farm –
Not as much fun as a John Wayne double feature,
Better than nothing – introducing us to writing
As a raison d'être, with his awkward charm.
Now that reminds me of a lunch in Manhattan –
Mainly a Greek salad – friends fighting
Over some toast and a plastic packet of grape
Jelly – in the recesses of the restaurant some rattan
Furniture reminded me of another life among 'Farm
Implements and Rutabagas in a Landscape',
A sestina that reminded me of a work by Nietzsche
Designed to inspire widespread fear and alarm
The way crowds flee from an alien creature.

Hollywood Story

Here's a rule of thumb – in Hollywood the villains
All have British accents – *Laura, North*
By Northwest – fans in their hundreds of millions
Watch, guzzling popcorn, in a trance
While actresses like Sally Field sally forth
To wrestle with their fate, trap some dumb hunk
Into marriage, honeymoon on the S.S. *France*
Where they sleep for six days and wake in Paris
Only to fall for a jazz trumpeter, some lunk
Like Paul Newman – no, Rip Torn –
But run off with a Pool Guy played by Richard Harris
Only to end up in Newark or South Bend,
Indiana, home of Indians – hoping to be reborn
Or at least born again before THE inevitable END.

Sex and Money

How to end up with half a million bucks?
Easy: invest a million in publishing verse.
Set up an investors' meeting. Wear a tux.
Explain that the rhyme scheme saves you from the curse
That fells the careless funds manager at his desk,
The team leader boozing on his holiday boat.
Investment's a faith, an existential risk
That touches the blade of the present to your throat.
The past's a printed plot, but the future's a worry.
In autumn the major banks should conglomerate.
Teams of managers rush about. Junior traders hurry.
Executives are told that should they accommodate
Their partners' particular sexual perversions,
Winter will resound to the sounds of physical exertions.

Mr Hyde

A, azure, B, brown, C, clatter,
Alphabet of failed endeavours,
What bankers use to attempt to flatter
The timid investor. Rainbows float in the sky
Above the gas lights. Dr Jekyll severs
The last thread that ties him to humanity
And plunges into his own id – a cry
That is almost a scream, nearly a groan,
As he treads the black brick road to insanity.
'Tread' is not right – capers and skips
To the tune of 'Merry Tod Malone',
Naked he is born, naked and alone he'll die –
In the brief in-between he has a song on his lips –
Far ahead, painful redemption, the eternal why.

Heroic Story

An unremarkable birth in a provincial town –
No talk of comets in the sky, or groaning wells –
A turbid adolescence. The academic gown,
That ocean of literature, freshets of verse,
All fodder. He learns to sell what sells,
Grows from dumb kid to something of a talker,
Picks up French, German, even Erse
'To read James Joyce in the original –'
Writing on baseball for the *New Yorker*,
Insists the plural of 'paradox' is 'conundra',
Boasts about sex while remaining virginal.
His articles on gastronomy touched the obscene.
Dying, he dreamed of that distant province: thunder,
Rain, everything over – what did it mean?

Poem Beginning with a Line by Kenneth Koch

This Connecticut landscape would have pleased Vermeer:
The pearly light that photographs the town,
The autumn blessing and the bitter cheer
Of winter close behind, with frosty crown.
The weekender lies abandoned for the week,
The den and sunroom vacant. On a couch,
The *New Yorker* open at a page that speaks
Of Aquascutum, Harris Tweed and scotch.
O Aquascutum, shield me from the blast,
And Harris Tweed, protect me from the cold.
As for scotch, let's leave it till the last
To warm my aching bones as I grow old.
Vermeer, to please his mistress, heard her sighs,
And painted pretty landscapes full of lies.

Another Poem Beginning with a Line by Kenneth Koch

This Connecticut landscape would have pleased Vermeer
The trash, the pickup truck, the cans of beer –
If only Vermeer hadn't been such a shit.
Oh well, it's hard for an artist to paint a hit –
To make the cut, to climb the greasy grade,
To make a real impression on the trade –
It's really hard, when you're totally pissed.
It isn't easy, when you've slit your wrist.
So fuck Connecticut and fuck Vermeer –
Who is this Dutchman with his can of cheer?
I'd rather look at Guston, or some Pollocks –
Who cares if the theory's mostly bollocks?
The landscape is really just a frame
For something that just sat there all the same.

Lost Weekend in Boca Raton

With a jug of hock and soda he gavottes –
Apres vous, Frau Frou-Frou – on the rantan,
Lurid feather duster with a two-can telephone,
Lurching from Can-Can deshabille to chi-chi spiv –
At fan-tan, the standard deviation too risque –
Cancel client's letter of last resort –
Earnings bonus payout glut provides
San Simian, pleasure dome of the Great Ape:
The caves of ice shaking with light, then toxic
Euphoria of libraries in Horrid Florida
Vying with the Master of the Susurrating Cymbal.
Eat canteen flummery, guzzle eau de Nil,
Now teach the Rat's Mouth Rotary Club a
Sarabande for sailors, the Romantic flaw.

747 Sonnet

A, tint of ash, pastel grey
And pale amber flakes, E, a feast
Of emerald ice-blocks at the break of day
When blood and gold tincture the mystic East.
I, less an order, more a hint
Of eau de Nil, flavours the local square
Where cobblestones hacked from the local flint
Bear a skin of ice that dazzles the air.
O for a beaker full of the warm South
Where tourists faint in the sticky Roman heat
And U offer purple promises of love
To be redeemed the next time we meet.
Qantas perfects its algorithm for seat yield;
a truck dumps rakes and shovels onto a field.

Spork

There I was, trying to eat a slippery noodle
And trying not to think of A, pink,
And E floating in a brick-red sink,
While Doris was gobbling down an Apple Strudel
With her right hand and a spork, a doodle
Leaking from her left hand, in blue ink
On a legal pad encased in a smelly mink
Legal pad case. Meanwhile her poodle –
With its 'I for Corn Silk' collar and lead
Had urinated on the art-deco linoleum
To the discomfort of the fussy waiter
(O for his navy blue jacket!) – a breed
(U, the leaf-green cans of raw petroleum)
with urinary problems that were much worse later.

Nitrile

A, blue gloves made of Nitrile,
Tougher than the usual kitchen kit.
Princess E for Egotism, her tight smile,
Migraine and 'glass empty' gloom fit.
I for Ivy League, dark green
And gold ribbon, chaps training
To be chaps, clearly heard, hardly seen,
O for Oblique Orange, windy, raining
In the city U plan to visit soon.
The train screeches to a halt, of course.
Check the coloured files. It's a thrill
To see the pairing: bride marries groom.
A trader suicides, in the Bourse.
Throw away the gloves. Take your pill.

Dental Adhesive

A, peppermint green, the colour of pain
In the dentist's chair as he finishes injecting;
E, pastel blue, colour of novocaine
That isolates the thinking, suffering I,
Colour of a two-part adhesive protecting
An ageing human from the human race,
At least those who practise an eye for an eye,
And the dental traders who swap a tooth for a tooth.
Those lessons born of suffering, that useless grace –
They turn a would-be philosopher into a clown,
A man as old as sin, who thinks of youth
As a state recently and reluctantly foregone,
But that was middle age – O, brown,
U, black – that brings us all undone.

Plum Tree

A, pink, gums and slobber, baby text,
Spun sugar on a stick, fluffy, light;
E, plum, tree like a wedding dress, white
For one brief season, blood red the next;
I, champagne, now you look a fright
Guzzling from a flute, flirting with your ex,
Hoping to end up on the carpet, horrid sex,
Torrent of regret to the end of the night.
O, blue, twilight dreams, when the sour
Beams of the sinking sun through the cocktail hour
Illuminate what's in your glass, futile blend,
Failing day, wreckage; U, green,
God of jealousy and the unclean,
Coming at last to an appalling end.

Tasman Sonnet

A, green, the tint of absinthe dripping through
A wad of lawn clippings – E,
Chartreuse, colour that only monks can see –
I, cloudy violet with sparkling points of blue
Or paler, the fresh paint sheen of a car –
When new, easy to buy – old, hard to sell.
O, orange, the sound of a tolling bell
Travelling over town and factory, very far –
U, under clear water, underwear –
Your flight spoiled by lots of crying babies
Though all of Europe is reflected in your eyes.
You think you hear, as you brush your hair,
The howling of a kennel full of hounds with rabies.
A rainbow as you land; then a career surprise.

Mouton Cadet

E, bronze, I, salmon, O, green, A, tangerine:
A heap of Florida clementines, on the stool
Where a slab of fish on a bed of ice is growing cool,
According to what's written in the culinary magazine
Featuring the statue of an ancient king, his rule
Likened by historians to the flat, calm green
Of a bowling lawn. Canute? Better heard than seen,
Stamping and shouting at the ocean like a fool.
These heaving salty irruptions slowly grow calm.
U, cadet blue. He wipes the ink-stain from his palm.
His descendant signed the Magna Carta, it is said.
Cadet, a younger sheep, an educated boor,
Thoroughly trained in the complicated arts of war,
Wearing his uniform, the dove grey suited to the dead.

Crowded Hour

A, Tangerine, lipstick 1962, daring
Hint of flame and wild behaviour,
E, lemon, sour surprise and rave, your
Suspicious self out for a welcome airing
On Fifth Avenue, your midday saviour
A transparent fellow spirit, the caring
Caress of a martini smoothly preparing
Your conscience to accept a second favour –
Bartender's gift of one half-empty bottle –
I, corn silk hair, love at full throttle,
O, blue shadows, delicate gloom
Pricked with traffic lights in the evening air –
U, olive green of underwater hair –
Scuba, the acronym, in the crowded room.

Detour

A, hot pink, babies angry when kissed,
Gummy smile clenching to a scowl,
E, snow blessing the street, a lisped vowel
Hiding midnight's infidelities, the wife pissed,
Smile (angelic) changing to grimace (foul),
Faint flutter of pulse at the wrist
As the Grim Reaper calls with his damned list.
I, sallow salmon, time to throw in the towel
and get outta here. O, tropical jungle green,
U, blue, lavender, dizzy aquamarine –
Padding from the pool, dripping wet, past
Croaking frogs, pythons, hamburger joints
Covered in vines, then a sign in Chinese that points
To the busy city – lights, people – home at last.

Far North Farm

A, silver, E, snow, U, dead-leaf green:
Spoons with sugar and dripping water, hillocks of snow
Traversed by hopeful young men with a moneyed glow
And sleds and perspiration, silver-blue clouds again
Chilling the horizon, a thousand miles to go.
Leave these 'adventurers', laughing in between
Signing media deals and muttering something obscene.
Schoolboys worship them, writing out a motto
In Latin, about suffering and stiff upper lips.
I, salmon sandwiches and hot chips.
O, the empty bottle is the colour of fear.
Push on. You'll make it home, at dawn.
Who cares that you look a right prawn,
Sipping absinthe in the Pub with No Beer.

The Good Ship Lollipop

A, pink, E, bronze, I, bisque, U, blue: lips
Like ice cream, gaze mirror-breaking Medusa
Versus the world, diary notes of looser
Prose curses and bad faith and paper clips.
On set two days the director tried to goose her.
Some nautical epic, sailors, songs, ships
With lots of ribbons and a truckload of gawking VIPs
From downtown, one old biddy like a moose, her
Jowls trembling. But none of that matters
To our heroine, glowing in the mirror that flatters:
O, green, fandom fizzes in her head.
So it should! The sky Polaroid blue, ocean lime green,
That god-like actor murmuring something obscene.
today sparkles with life. Long enough dead.

Weasels

A grey, U dun, O clear: flattering
Tones that echo in the mind for perhaps a day,
Coloured blocks clattering under children's play,
Clouds dispersing at a breath, window panes shattering:
E, a new building down town painted a flattering
Shade of mint; echoes in empty classrooms, girls, grey
Uniforms, a gathered apron full of pearls, so they say;
I, grey-blue, rocks and gravel, rainwater splattering...
In winter, rain falling on a hail-shrouded lawn:
U, old Army underwear, weasels fast asleep
Under the grass: lumps, cloddy tranche;
O, a windows washer pauses and sobs, born
On the Fourth of July but now just another creep,
Acres of glass breaking in an earthquake, avalanche!

The Consonants

B, brave brown, C, icicle
Pendant, D, dun though pale,
F for faint mauve, fish and bicycle,
G, gothic paint in a green pail
H, an ambulance red and white,
J, lemon rain, K, snakebite,
L, bandage around M for kill,
N, no concrete freeway crush thrill,
P, torrid personals, Q for Quimper,
R, pale reptile, Sun and beach
And T-shirts, V, abrasive screech
Where a red vixen might scamper.
X is just black, Y mottled spoon,
Z pale grey sleeping under the moon.

Fashion

Why
are these
short,
clipped lines
in
fashion?

They
stretch out
a whim
to the
length of a
passion.

Notes to the Poems

Venue and sometimes date of publication is listed herein.

The poems in Section One, from 'Algernon Limattsia' (p.13) to 'That Greenish Flower' (p.72), are loosely derived from some poems in *The Best of the Best American Poetry* (*BBAP*), 25th Anniversary Edition, Robert Pinsky, Editor; David Lehman, Series Editor. Scribner: New York, 2013.

The poems in Section Two, from 'Variations on a Theme of E.P. (Elias Pfenning)' (p.75) to 'Fly' (p.97), are loosely derived from some poems in *The Open Door: One Hundred Poems, One Hundred Years of 'Poetry' Magazine* (*TOD*). Don Share and Christian Wiman, Eds. Chicago: University of Chicago Press, 2012.

The poems from 'Abjure' (p.122) to 'The Consonants' (p.136) are sonnets, mostly though not always rhymed.

Page 13, 'Algernon Limattsia' began as a draft using the end-words of 'Terminal Nostalgia' by Sherman Alexie (who identifies as a Native American), *The Best of the Best American Poetry* (*BBAP*), page 1. The title is an anagram of 'Terminal Nostalgia'. Published in *New American Writing* No 32, 2014.

p.14, 'My Sister' began as a draft using the end-words of 'Soft Money' by Rae Armantrout. *BBAP* 23. Published in *Vlak* magazine (contemporary poetics and the arts), Prague, 2015.

p.15, 'The Puma in the Duma' began as a draft using the end-words of 'Wakefulness' by John Ashbery. *BBAP* 25. Published in *Australian Book Review*, October 2014.

p.16, 'Robed With the Cloth of Gold' began as a draft using the end-words of 'Bored' by Margaret Atwood. 'Bored' is an anagram of 'Robed'. *BBAP* 27.

p.18, 'In Junction Junction' began as a draft using the end-words of 'Injunction' by Frank Bidart. *BBAP* 29.

p.19, 'Intuition' began as a draft using the end-words of 'Feminine Intuition' by Stephanie Brown. *BBAP* 30.

p.20, 'The Animals' began as a draft using some of the end-words of 'The Life of Towns' by Anne Carson. *BBAP* 34.

p.23, 'Three Lemons' began as a draft using the end-words of 'Three Oranges' by Charles Bukowski. *BBAP* 32. Published in *Southerly* magazine, 2015.

p.24, 'Small Town' began as a draft using some of the end-words of 'The Life of Towns' by Anne Carson. *BBAP* 34.

p.26, 'A Pompeiian Aristocrat Considers the Future' began as a draft using the end-words of 'Self-portrait as Four Styles of Pompeian Wall Painting' by Henri Cole. *BBAP* 47. Published in *Southerly* magazine, 2015.

p.28, 'Family' began as a draft using the end-words of 'En Famille' by Robert Creeley. *BBAP* 52.

p.30, 'God Goes to Work' began as a draft using the end-words of 'Dharma' by Billy Collins, *BBAP* 50.

p.31, 'A Nipping and an Eager Air' began as a draft using the end-words of 'You Art A Scholar, Horatio, Speak To It' by Olena Kalytiak Davis. *BBAP* 55.

p.32, 'Regeneration' began as a draft using the end-words of 'Our Generation' by Carl Dennis. *BBAP* 58.

p.33, 'Bare Skin' began as a draft using the end-words of 'Skin' by Susan Dickman. *BBAP* 60.

p.34, 'The Parkas' began as a draft using the end-words of 'Desire' by Stephen Dobyns. *BBAP* 62. Published in *Eleven Eleven* at the MFA Program, California College of the Arts, San Francisco, November 2014.

p.36, 'Doting on Blubber' began as a draft using the end-words of 'Difference' by Mark Doty. *BBAP* 65. Published in *New American Writing* No 32, 2014.

p.38, 'All Souls College' began as a draft using the end-words of 'All Souls'' by Rita Dove. *BBAP* 68.

p.39, 'A Man and a Woman' began as a draft using the end-words of 'The Imagined' by Stephen Dunn. *BBAP* 72. Published in *Oz-Burp*, Donnithorne Street Press, Melbourne Vic 2014.

p.40, 'How it Starts' began as a draft using the end-words of 'How it Will End' by Denise Duhamel. *BBAP* 70.

p.42, 'Never Safe' began as a draft using the end-words of 'Safe' by Linda Gregerson. *BBAP* 84.

p.45, 'Congress, the State of Mind' began as a draft using the end-words of 'Powers of Congress' by Alice Fulton. *BBAP* 73.

p.46, 'Fernando's Hideaway' began as a draft using the end-words of 'Salutations to Fernando Pessoa' by Allen Ginsberg. *BBAP* 74.

p.48, 'Pesca Land' began as a draft using the end-words of 'Landscape' by Louise Glück. *BBAP* 76. The title is an anagram of 'Landscape'.

p.50, The Manifest' began as a draft using the end-words of 'Manifest Destiny' by Jorie Graham. *BBAP* 78.

p.55, 'Borodino' began as a draft using the end-words of 'The War' by Linda Gregg. *BBAP* 88.

p.56, 'American Prophecy' began as a draft using the end-words of 'Prophecy' by Donald Hall. *BBAP* 91.

p.60, 'Boston Café' began as a draft using the end-words of 'Cafeteria in Boston' by Thom Gunn. *BBAP* 89.

p.61, 'Picking on the Oil Company' began as a draft using the end-words of 'Having Intended to Merely Pick on an Oil Company, the Poem Goes Awry' by Bob Hicok. *BBAP* 108. Published in *Vlak* magazine (contemporary poetics and the arts), Prague, 2015.

p.62, 'One Night in Nam' began as a draft using the end-words of 'Facing It' by Yusef Komunyakaa. *BBAP* 132. Published in *Vlak* magazine (contemporary poetics and the arts), Prague, 2015.

p.63, 'Baby Weather' began as a draft using the end-words of 'Past all Understanding' by Heather McHugh. *BBAP* 146.

p.64, 'Engagement Ring Cycle' began as a draft using the end-words of 'The 'Ring' Cycle' by James Merrill. *BBAP* 152.

p.67, 'The Animal Generation' began as a draft using the end-words of 'There will be Animals' by Thylias Moss. *BBAP* 159.

p.68, 'Hateful Mail' began as a draft using the end-words of 'Hate Mail' by Carol Muskie-Dukes. *BBAP* 167.

p.69, 'Q and A' began as a draft using the end-words of 'Q' by Sharon Olds. *BBAP* 169. Published in *Vlak* magazine (contemporary poetics and the arts), Prague, 2015.

p.70, 'At Arles' began as a draft using the end-words of 'The Window at Arles' by Megan O'Rourke. *BBAP* 170.

p.72, 'That Greenish Flower' began as a draft using the end-words of 'Asphodel' by Alicia E. Stallings. *BBAP* 211. Published in *Vlak* magazine (contemporary poetics and the arts), Prague, 2015.

p.75, 'Variations on a Theme of E.P. (Elias Pfenning)' began as a draft using the end-words of 'In a Station of the Metro' by Ezra Pound. *The Open Door: One Hundred Poems, One Hundred Years of 'Poetry' Magazine* (*TOD*) page 21.

p.76, 'The Linden Tree' began as a draft using the end-words of 'Anti-Romantic' by Marie Ponsot. *TOD* 23. Published in *Overland*, Melbourne, 2015.

p.77, 'Young Folly' began as a draft using the end-words of 'The Young' by Roddy Lumsden. *TOD* 24. Published in *Overland*, Melbourne, 2015.

p.78, 'The Tyrant Eros' began as a draft using the end-words of 'Eros Turannos' by Edwin Arlington Robinson. *TOD* 27.

p.80, 'Dog's Life' began as a draft using the end-words of 'It was a Bichon Frisé's Life...' by Ange Mlinko. *TOD* 29.

p.81, 'The Search' began as a draft using the end-words of 'Song' by Muriel Rukeyser. *TOD* 30.

p.82, 'Your Life' began as a draft using the end-words of 'The Hereafter' by August Kleinzahler. *TOD* 31. Published in *Australian Book Review* in 2015.

p.84, 'Look at my Parents, Will You?' began as a draft using the end-words of 'Look' by Laura Kasischke. *TOD* 39.

p.85, 'One Variation' began as a draft using the end-words of 'from 'Eight Variations'' by Weldon Kees. *TOD* 40.

p.86, 'Older than Forty' began as a draft using the end-words of 'Men at Forty' by Donald Justice. *TOD* 54.

p.87, 'Man With Banjo' began as a draft using the end-words of 'O Daedalus, Fly Away Home' by Robert Hayden. *TOD* 83.

p.88, 'Me and My Landscape' began as a draft using the end-words of 'My Chosen Landscape' by P.K. Page. *TOD* 59.

p.90. 'Et in California Ego' began as a draft using the end-words of 'On visiting a Borrowed Country House in Arcadia', by Alicia E. Stallings. *TOD* 48. Published in *Cordite* magazine in November 2014.

p.92. 'In Plato's Bed' began as a draft using the end-words of 'In the Naked Bed, in Plato's Cave' by Delmore Schwartz. *TOD* 52.

p.93. 'Show Us at the Ming Place' began as a draft using the end-words of 'Mingus at the Showplace' by William Matthews. *TOD* 53.

p.94. 'Meditation at Breakfast' began as a draft using the end-words of 'Meditation on a Grapefruit' by Craig Arnold. *TOD* 57. Published in *Oz-Burp*, Donnithorne Street Press, Melbourne Vic 2014.

p.95. 'Coffee at the Palace of the Great Hoon' began as a draft using the end-words of 'Tea at the Palaz of Hoon' by Wallace Stevens. *TOD* 63. Published in *Cordite Poetry Review* in 2014, at http://cordite.org.au/.

p.96. 'Tomb in the Rain' began as a draft using the end-words of 'At Melville's Tomb' by Hart Crane. *TOD* 82.

p.97. 'Fly' began as a draft using the end-words of 'The Lie' by Don Paterson. *TOD* 146.

p.101, 'Cold Spring' is a 'quintet' derived from Richard Yates, *Cold Spring Harbour*. New York, 1986: Dell Publishing. The form 'quintet' was invented by myself, and consists of taking a novel and typing out five of the author's sentences: the first and last ones, and any three other sentences, usually spaced more or less evenly through the text. Lineation is added to form a poem.

p.101, 'Power' is a quintet derived from Graham Greene, *The Power and the Glory*.

p.102, 'Quiet' is a quintet derived from Graham Greene, *The Quiet American*.

p.102, 'Heaven' is a quintet derived from Graham Greene, *Travels with My Aunt*.

p.103, 'The Rats' is a quintet derived from A.J.A. Symons, *The Quest for Corvo*.

p.103, 'Honor' is a quintet derived from Graham Greene, *The Honorary Consul*.

p.104, 'Variations and Reverse Mazurka' is based on the eight ten-line rhymed stanzas of John Keats' 1819 poem 'Ode to a Nightingale'. The poem begins with a line from Keneth Koch's poem 'Fresh Air' quoted by Stephen Burt in an article titled 'Close Calls with Nonsense: how to read, and perhaps enjoy, very new poetry' as follows: 'Despite the achievements of very famous modernists (T. S. Eliot, William Carlos Williams), by the mid-1950s most American poetry seemed predictable, passé; its elaborate stanzas reflected the safety of professors' lives. (Kenneth Koch epitomized and parodied their output in one line: "This Connecticut landscape would have pleased Vermeer.")'. Published in *Island* magazine, Hobart, 2015.

p.107, 'Five Egyptian Pieces' are all derived from the official English transla-
tion of a speech by French Foreign Minister D. De Villepin in Cairo, Egypt, 2003
(Speech by Mr Domenique de Villepin, Minister of Foreign Affairs for France,
Cairo, 12 April 2003: 'The Mediterranean World and the Middle East'.) In the case
of each poem, most of the words of M Villepin's speech were removed, and the
remainder, in the same order as they appeared in the speech, made up the poem.
All five poems were first published in the magazine *la Traductière*, Paris, in June
2007, as part of the thirtieth Festival Franco-Anglais de Poésie. Also published in
Cordite Poetry Review, August no. 47 2014.

p.109, 'Least Said' is a reply to a poem by John Ashbery ('Feel Free') published
in the November 2011 issue of *Australian Book Review*; the two poems were
published side by side. The last word of each line of John Ashbery's poem is used
as the last word of each line of 'Least Said'. The title is a completion of the title
of John Ashbery's earlier poem 'Soonest Mended'; together they make up the
folk saying 'Least said, soonest mended.' 'Joy H. Breshan' is an anagram of 'John
Ashbery'.

p.110, 'Manacles' was written in Cambridge UK.

p.113, 'Rubies' is a poem in free verse. 'rubes': country bumpkins, 'della bosco',
'from the woods, woodlands' (Italian). Cf. English 'bosky', wooded.

p.114, 'Four Variations on a Poem by Pam Brown.' Each sonnet consists of two
different Petrachan quartets with a non-standard rhymed sestet.

p.117, 'Adjectivitis at Lagunitas' is a version of a poem by US poet Robert Hass,
'Meditations at Lagunitas', 1987. First published in *Van Gogh's Ear*, 2008, ed.
Dawn-Michelle Baude.

p.118, 'Loxodrome' is dedicated to poet Ken Bolton.   ¶ the sunset / says
something lurid against a shop window] refers to 'the sky to the west was glow-
ing / like the windows full of Italian furniture / & thanks to its low rent coloratura
/ or a style suggesting its own collapse / for a moment I felt le sang des poètes',
John Forbes, 'Serenade'.   ¶ Sir Francis Bacon] '...in March 1626, driving one
day near Highgate [a district to the north of London] and deciding on impulse
to discover whether snow would delay the process of putrefaction, he stopped
his carriage, purchased a hen, and stuffed it with snow. He was seized with a
sudden chill, which brought on bronchitis, and he died at the Earl of Arundel's
house nearby on April 9, 1626.' – *Encyclopedia Britannica* 2004 Deluxe Edition
CD.   ¶ Charlie Parker] Among various and sometimes dubious explanations of
jazz musician Charlie Parker's nickname 'Yardbird' is the following: 'Parker's fa-
mous nickname, "Yardbird", came from an incident when the band's bus ran over
a chicken. The bus driver stopped and Parker retrieved the bird and later had it
cooked by his landlady.' <http://charlie-parkero.tripod.com/id12.html>.   ¶ Title]
loxodrome [back-formation from *loxodromic*, from Gk. *loxos*, oblique + *dromos*,
course] a rhumb line, a curve that appears to be a straight line on a Mercator-pro-
jection map, an imaginary line on the earth's surface cutting all meridians at the

same angle, used as the standard method of plotting a ship's course on a chart. First published in *Rabbit* magazine number 11, Australia, early 2014.

p.122, 'Abjure' is an unrhymed sonnet; that is, a free verse poem of fourteen lines. First published in *The Australian*, June 2012.

p.122, 'Opus Plus' is a free-verse sonnet with truncated lines.

p.123, 'Poem Beginning With a Line by Bunting' is a Shakespearean sonnet. See later extensive note on Bunting. Alert readers will have noted that some of the sonnets following are loosely based on the concept behind Arthur Rimbaud's 'Voyelles' sonnet dealing with the supposed colours of the vowels (*un sonnet en alexandrins d'Arthur Rimbaud écrit à Paris dans les premiers mois de 1872, Wikipedia*), though with a more variegated palette. It should be noted here that Rimbaud chose to sequence the vowels AEIUO, not AEIOU as it usually is in French and in English, perhaps to coincide with the Biblical quote 'I am the Alpha and the Omega'. Metrically, most of the sonnets in this book are loosely in iambic pentameter.

p.123, 'The Year my Shadow Pagoda Lost its Savage Home' a free verse sonnet which uses all the words that Australian poet Pam Brown claimed (in 2013) should never be used in a poem or book title: pagoda, shadow, year, lost, savage, home, miracle, archaeology, unsung, paradise, paradox, dark, heroes. Published in *Intertia Magazine*, USA.

p.124, 'The Hairdresser' is a Spencerian sonnet, a form invented by English poet Edmund Spenser as an outgrowth of the nine-line stanza pattern he used in his book-length poem 'The Faerie Queene' (a b a b b c b c c), and has the pattern a b a b b c b c c d c d e e. First published in *Steamer*, Australia, June 2013.

p.124, 'The Love Song of J. Edgar Hoover' follows the rhyme scheme and (roughly) the metrical scheme of Pushkin's 'Onegin' sonnet form, of which *Wikipedia* says is 'the verse form popularized (or invented) by the Russian poet Alexander Pushkin through his novel in verse *Eugene Onegin*. The work was mostly written in verses of iambic tetrameter with the rhyme scheme a B a B c c D D e F F e G G, where the lowercase letters represent feminine endings (i.e., with an additional unstressed syllable) and the uppercase representing masculine ending (i.e. stressed on the final syllable).' The supposition that J. Edgar Hoover was secretly a cross-dresser or was gay (or both) has a weird aptness, but it is probably untrue. Line 9: couch and fescue] two varieties of lawn grass. Couch is pronounced 'cooch'. First published in *The Australian*, February 2012. Published in *The Battersea Review*, London, ed. Ben Mazer, July 2013. Published on *The Best American Poetry* blog at http://blog.bestamericanpoetry.com/the_best_ameri-can_poetry/. Published in the chapbook *Ten Sonnets*, Vagabond Press, Sydney and Tokyo, September 2013.

p.125, 'Poem Beginning with a line by John Anderson' is a Shakespearean sonnet. John Anderson was an Australian poet, 1948–1997. The poem was written while listening to a paper on his poetry given by Ella O'Keefe at the University of Auckland in March 2012.   ¶ Jindyworobaks] 'The Jindyworobak Movement was a nationalistic Australian literary movement whose white members sought to promote Indigenous Australian ideas and customs, particularly in poetry. They were active from the 1930s to around the 1950s. The movement intended to combat the influx of "alien" culture, which was threatening local art.' – *Wikipedia*. Published in The Melbourne *Age,* 2012. Published in the chapbook *Ten Sonnets,* Vagabond Press, Sydney and Tokyo, September 2013.

p.125, 'Postcard From Ischia' follows the rhyme scheme of the Onegin sonnet. Published in *Southerly* magazine in 2012.

p.126, 'Hark' This poem is in a rhyme scheme of my own invention – let's call it the Tranterian sonnet – rhyming a b a c b d c e d f e g f g. It uses phrases taken from the *Sydney Morning Herald* newspaper during August 2013, phrases that were occasionally modified. Published in *Rabbit* magazine in 2013.

p.126, 'The Creature' is another Tranterian sonnet. I had long wished to use the bilingual rhyme 'Nietzsche / creature'.

p.127, 'Hollywood Story' is another Tranterian sonnet.

p.127, 'Sex and Money' is a Shakespearean sonnet.

p.128, 'Mr Hyde'. 'On his Tod' is Cockney rhyming slang for 'On his Tod Malone', 'on his own'. Published in *Otoliths* magazine in 2013.

p.128, 'Heroic Story' is a Tranterian sonnet. Published in the *Harvard Review,* 2013. Published on *The Best American Poetry* blog at http://blog.bestamericanpoetry.com/the_best_american_poetry/. Published in the chapbook *Ten Sonnets,* Vagabond Press, Sydney and Tokyo, September 2013.

p.129, 'Poem Beginning with a Line by Kenneth Koch' is a Shakespearean sonnet which begins with the same line from Koch's poem 'Fresh Air' used in 'Variations and Reverse Mazurka' on page 104. Published in *Mascara* magazine in 2012.

p.129, 'Another Poem Beginning with a Line by Kenneth Koch' is in pentameter rhyming couplets, that is, heroic couplets. Published in *Mascara* magazine in 2012.

p.130, 'Lost Weekend in Boca Raton' is a sonnet crudely in the manner of US poet Wallace Stevens, and is in free verse, though in the form of a double reverse acrostic: the first letter of each line spells out the name Wallace Stevens, and the last letter of each line spells out the name in reverse order.   ¶ San Simian] 'Publishing baron William Randolph Hearst... inspired the forlorn millionaire of [the movie] *Citizen Kane*—thanks to a feud with filmmaker Orson Welles. [His]most famous [home] is undoubtedly Hearst Castle, a hilltop compound constructed on oceanfront ranch land Hearst had inherited from his mother near San Simeon, Calif. Architect Julia Morgan [...] was enlisted to design the 90,000-square-foot compound. Once complete, the sprawling personal palace contained 56 bedrooms, 61 bathrooms, 19 entertaining rooms, indoor and outdoor tiled swimming pools, tennis courts, a private movie theater, an airfield, the world's largest private zoo, and 127 acres of gardens. Constructed over a period of nearly thirty years, from 1919 to 1947, and never truly completed, the extravagant private home cost Hearst upwards of $500M in today's dollars. The Hearst Corporation donated the estate to the state of California, which now operates it as a museum.' [From: http://curbed.com/tags/hearst-castle] Published in *Southerly* magazine in 2014.

p.130, '747 Sonnet' I believe Pam Brown named this type of sonnet as the kind of poem written by an English Department academic scholar on the flight home from a sabbatical break 'overseas', that is, anywhere outside of Australia. In fact this poem was written in a Boeing 747 passenger jet en route from Sydney to Los Angeles. It uses the rhyme scheme of the Shakespearean sonnet, though the acute reader may note that lines 9 and 11 fail to rhyme. Published in the Melbourne *Age*, 2013. Published in the *Battersea Review* London in 2013. Published as a broadside poem by Desmond Kon at Squircle Press in Singapore in 2013. Published in the chapbook *Ten Sonnets,* Vagabond Press, Sydney and Tokyo, September 2013.

p.131, 'Spork' is a Petrachian sonnet, type 1.

p.131, 'Nitrile' begins as a Shakespearean sonnet, and after the octet utilises a Petrachan sestet. Published in *Southerly* magazine in 2013; also in *Battersea Review* London in 2013.

p.132, 'Dental Adhesive' is a Tranterian sonnet. Published in the Melborne *Age*, 2015.

p.132, 'Plum Tree' uses the rhyme scheme of Rimbaud's 'Voyelles' sonnet: a b b a b a a b c c d e e d. The conceit of the ornamental plum tree's marital colour change is taken from a poem by New Zealand writer Janet Frame.

p.133, 'Tasman Sonnet' has a modified Petrarchan octet with a Petrarchan sestet. Published in the *Times Literary Supplement* in June 2013. Published in the chapbook *Ten Sonnets,* Vagabond Press, Sydney and Tokyo, September 2013.

p.133, 'Mouton Cadet' uses the rhyme scheme of Rimbaud's 'Voyelles' sonnet. Published in the *Times Literary Supplement* in June 2013.

p.134, 'Crowded Hour', rhyme scheme ditto. Published in the *Best Australian Poems* anthology in 2013. Published in the *Times Literary Supplement* in June 2013. Published on *The Best American Poetry* blog at http://blog.bestamericanpoetry.com/the_best_american_poetry/. Published in the chapbook *Ten Sonnets,* Vagabond Press, Sydney and Tokyo, September 2013.

p.134, 'Detour', rhyme scheme ditto. Published in *The Australian* 2013. Published in the *Battersea Review* London in 2013. Published on *The Best American Poetry* blog at http://blog.bestamericanpoetry.com/the_best_american_poetry/. Published in the chapbook *Ten Sonnets,* Vagabond Press, Sydney and Tokyo, September 2013.

p.135, 'Far North Farm', rhyme scheme ditto. Published in the *Times Literary Supplement* in June 2013. Published on *The Best American Poetry* blog at http://blog.bestamericanpoetry.com/the_best_american_poetry/. Published in the chapbook *Ten Sonnets,* Vagabond Press, Sydney and Tokyo, September 2013.

p.135, 'The Good Ship Lollipop', rhyme scheme ditto. Published in the *North-East Review* Boston in 2013.

p.136, 'Weasels' is a Petrachan sonnet type 1. Published in the *North-East Review* Boston in 2013.

p.136, 'The Consonants' has the rhyme scheme of Onegin sonnet. Published in the *Best Australian Poems* anthology in 2013. Published in *Australian Book Review,*

2013. Published on *The Best American Poetry* blog at http://blog.bestamericanpo-etry.com/the_best_american_poetry/. Published in the chapbook *Ten Sonnets*, Vagabond Press, Sydney and Tokyo, September 2013.

p.137, 'Fashion' is a rhyming couplet with truncated lines. Published in the *Sydney Morning Herald*, September 2012.

Bunting: The sonnet titled 'Poem Beginning With a Line by Bunting' (page 123) was first published in the Melbourne *Age* on 3 March 2012, and later published in the chapbook *Ten Sonnets*, Vagabond Press, Sydney and Tokyo, September 2013. Like many of Shakespeare's sonnets, on which it is modelled, it's obscure, and for that it requires a note: my apologies.

The focus of the poem is British poet Basil Bunting, 1900-1985. He was born in Northumberland in Northern England, and developed non-conformist Quaker be-liefs, a thick Northern brogue and a Northerner's distrust of 'southrons' (English people from the south of the North.) He spent a traumatic year in prison in 1918 as a conscientious objector, and later travelled widely. Bunting's poetry began to show the influence of Ezra Pound, whom he had befriended in the 1920s. He visit-ed Pound in Rapallo, Italy, and later settled there with his family from 1931 to 1933.

During World War II, Bunting served in British Military Intelligence in Persia under cover of working as a journalist for *The Times*, and after the war he con-tinued to serve on the British Embassy staff in Tehran until he was expelled by Muhammad Mussadegh (or Mossadeq) in 1952. He was active in stirring up mob violence and demonstrations against Mossadeq, who had been elected Prime Min-ister of Iran in 1951 by the Parliament of Iran by a democratic vote of 79 to 12.

Bunting was part of the plot engineered by the CIA, MI6 and Anglo Oil to depose Mossadeq, whose administration, as *Wikipedia* says, 'introduced a wide range of social reforms but is most notable for its nationalization of the Iranian oil industry, which had been under British control since 1913 through the Anglo-Per-sian Oil Company (APOC/AIOC) (later British Petroleum or BP).' They go on to say that he 'was removed from power in a coup on 19 August 1953, organised and carried out by the United States CIA at the request of the British MI6.' Soon Shah Pahlevi and the CIA-trained SAVAK, his repressive secret police force, took power.

Wikipedia says 'The coup is widely believed to have significantly contributed to anti-American sentiment in Iran and the Middle East. The 1979 Iranian Revolution deposed the Shah and replaced the pro-Western dictatorship with the largely an-ti-Western Islamic Republic of Iran.' That's the Iran regime that, over thirty years later, was keen to build nuclear weapons and 'wipe Israel from the map'.

Back in Newcastle, Bunting worked as a journalist on a local paper until he was rediscovered a decade later by the young poet Tom Pickard, who encouraged him to continue writing. In 1965, he published his long poem 'Briggflatts', named for the Quaker meeting house in Cumbria where he is now buried. Unlike all his earlier work, which met a muted response, 'Briggflats' enjoyed an immediate success among a new generation of writers and readers.

I go on at length about Bunting because, though he had a brief fame in the 1960s and 1970s, when many young poets came under his influence, his floruit as an important writer was relatively brief, and he has now been dead for nearly thirty years. Beside his mentor Pound, whose huge fame cast its shadow over half a century, Bunting is a minor figure with not much to say, and there are many poets today who have not heard of him.

Where can you find out more about Bunting? *Jacket* magazine has a brief feature on his work, as well as a link to a recording of Bunting reading a short poem, 'At Briggflatts Meetinghouse' (1975). The poem begins:

Boasts time mocks cumber Rome. Wren
set up his own monument.
Others watch fells dwindle, think
the sun's fires sink.

I have borrowed from the poem's first line for my poem. In *Jacket* magazine on the Internet you can read a translation of that first line into standard southern English, kindly provided by the late Richard Caddel, then a Director of the Basil Bunting Poetry Centre at Durham University:

– 'Boasts (noun, plural) [at which] time mocks [en]cumber Rome'; or,

– 'The boasts which Rome once made about its permanence now encumber it, and are mocked by the passage of time'.

– 'Wren' is Sir Christopher Wren, 1632-1723, English architect and professor of astronomy at Oxford.

The second line of my poem ('Roasts thyme scents set on ledge') echoes the first, though in a lighter key. A translation into plain English might run like this: 'Roasts (legs of roast lamb, or roasted chickens, perhaps) which the herb thyme has scented, are usually placed on a window-ledge to cool and to let the meat 'set', or become firm.'

The third line adverts to the ancient practice of singing rhyming hymns in St Paul's Cathedral (designed by Wren), hymns Bunting might well criticise as belonging to the official state religion of the 'southrons', the Church of England.

'Pound disposes' refers to the common motto 'Man proposes, God disposes', taken from a work in Latin by Thomas à Kempis. Pound's acolytes would have seen him as a master poet, and like a god of literature. As well the phrase 'humans merely err' adverts to the motto from Pope 'To Err is Human; to Forgive, Divine' (from Alexander Pope, 'Essay on Criticism' l.525, 1711) though that is based on earlier English sources and indeed appears in Latin: *humanum est errare*, it is human to err.

Lines seven and eight note the fact that Bunting could speak smooth English as well as any 'southron' when required, but slipped back into his Northern brogue to orate his poetry.

I think of the apparent ease with which Bunting slips into the role of servant of the English upper class as a spy for MI6 in Tehran, sipping cocktails at Embassy receptions and speaking with a fluent Southern English accent, eager to help destabilise an elected government at the behest of his masters, Anglo Oil, and I don't quite know how to judge him.

The only biography we had (in mid-2013) of Bunting is by Keith Aldritt. It poses some disturbing questions. At one point in Tehran, Bunting in his role of MI6 spy send an American woman to her death.

When she arrived in Isfahan, Basil, tipped off by the Russians, observed her and finally handed her over to the Americans. He thought that such a guileless, amateur spy would simply be told off and sent home to Chicago. He was horrified to learn, three days later, that the American Office of Strategic Services, the forerunner of the CIA, had shot her.

Readers may like to note that there is a more recent biography, *A Strong Song Tows Us: The Life of Basil Bunting* by Richard Burton (Infiniteideas, pp.608, £30, ISBN: 9781908984).

'Brag, tenor bull' is an adaptation of the opening of Bunting's famous long poem 'Briggflats' (the Rawthey is a river):

> Brag, sweet tenor bull,
> descant on Rawthey's madrigal,
> each pebble its part
> for the fells' late spring.